CLASSIC SERMONS
ON
SUFFERING

KREGEL CLASSIC SERMONS Series

CLASSIC SERMONS
ON
SUFFERING

Compiled by
Warren W. Wiersbe

KREGEL PUBLICATIONS
Grand Rapids, Michigan 49501

We acknowledge with appreciation the rights to use the
following copyrighted material:
"But When Life Tumbles in, What Then?" by Arthur John
Gossip and the four sermons by James S. Stewart on "God
and the Fact of Suffering" (chapters 5, 6, 7 and 8) used by
permission of T & T Clark, Edinburgh, Scotland. "Heaven's
Help for Troubled Hearts" by Walter A. Maier, used by
permission of Concordia Publishing House, St. Louis. "The
Right Use of Affliction" by John Calvin, used by permission
of William B. Eerdmans Publishing Co. and Baker Book
House, Grand Rapids. "When Worn With Sickness" by
William E. Sangster used by permission of the author's
son, Dr. Paul Sangster, North Yorkshire, England.

Library of Congress Cataloging-in-Publication Data

Classic Sermons on Suffering / compiled by Warren W.
Wiersbe.
     p.   cm.— (Kregel classic sermons series)
Includes index.

   1. Suffering—Religious aspects—Christianity—Sermons.
2. Sermons, English. I. Wiersbe, Warren W. II. Series:
Kregel classic sermons series.

BT732.7.C54   1984   248.8'6   84-11260
                                           CIP

ISBN   0-8254-4027-0 (pbk.)

3 4 5 6 7 Printing/Year 94 93 92 91 90

Printed in the United States of America

Dedicated with grateful appreciation
to the memory of

CHARLES W. KOLLER
(1896-1983)

known to the Church as a
gifted preacher and educator;

known to his students as an
inspirer of great preaching,
an encourager of devoted service,
and an exemplar of effective
pulpit and pastoral ministry.

"I thank my God upon every
remembrance of you" (Philippians 1:3)

CONTENTS

PREFACE

THE *CLASSIC SERMONS SERIES* is an attempt to assemble and publish meaningful sermons from master preachers about significant themes.

These are *sermons*, not essays or chapters taken from books about themes. Not all of these sermons could be called "great," but all of them are *meaningful.* They apply the truths of the Bible to the needs of the human heart, which is something that all effective preaching must do.

While some are better known than others, all of the preachers, whose sermons I have selected, had important ministries and were highly respected in their day. The fact that a sermon is included in this volume does not mean that either the compiler or the publisher agrees with or endorses everything that the man did, preached, or wrote. The sermon is here, because it has a valued contribution to make.

These are sermons about *significant* themes. The pulpit is no place to play with trivia. The preacher has thirty minutes in which to help mend broken hearts, change defeated lives, and save lost souls; and he can never accomplish this demanding ministry by distributing homiletical tid-bits. In these difficult days, we do not need "clever" pulpiteers who discuss the times; we need dedicated ambassadors who will preach the eternities.

The reading of these sermons can enrich your own spiritual life. The studying of them can enrich your own skills as an interpreter and expounder of God's truth. However God uses these sermons in your own life and ministry, my prayer is that His Church around the world will be encouraged and strengthened.

WARREN W. WIERSBE

But When Life Tumbles in, What Then?

Arthur John Gossip (1873-1954) preached
this sermon shortly after the sudden death of
his beloved wife. He ministered in Great
Britain as the pastor of four different
churches, as an army chaplain, and as a professor of Practical Theology at Trinity College,
Glasgow, Scotland. This sermon comes from
his book *The Hero in Thy Soul,* published in
1928 by T. & T. Clark, Edinburgh, Scotland.

Arthur John Gossip

1

BUT WHEN LIFE TUMBLES IN, WHAT THEN?

> If thou hast run with the footmen, and they have wearied thee, then how canst thou contend with horses? and if in the land of peace, wherein thou trustedst, they wearied thee, then how wilt thou do in the swelling of Jordan? (Jeremiah 12:5).

HERE IS A MAN who, musing upon the bewilderments of life, has burst into God's presence, hot, angry, stunned by His ordering of things, with a loud babble of clamorous protest. It is unfair, he cries, unfair! And frowningly he looks into the face of the Almighty. It is unfair! And then suddenly he checks himself, and putting this blunt question to it, feels his heart grow very still and very cold. For after all, he asks himself, what is it you have to complain about so far? Nothing that everybody does not share. Only the usual little rubs and frets and ills of life that fall to everyone, no more. And if these have broken through your guard, pushed aside your religion, made you so sour and peevish and cross towards God—God help you,—what will happen when, sudden as a shell screaming out of the night, one of the great crashing dispensations bursts in your life, and leaves an emptiness where there had been a home, a tumbled ruin of your ordered ways, a heart so sore you wonder how it holds together? If you have caught your breath, poor fool, when splashing through the shallow waters of some summer brook, how will you fare when Jordan bursts its banks, and rushes, far as the eye can see, one huge, wild swirl of angry waters, and, your feet caught away, half choked, you are tossed nearer and nearer to the roaring of the falls, and over it?

Suppose that, to you as to Job, suddenly, out of the blue, there leap dreadful tidings of disaster, would you have the grit to pull yourself together and to face it as he did? "The Lord gave, and the Lord hath taken away; blessed be the name of the Lord" (Job 1:21). Suppose that, to you as to Ezekiel, that valiant soul, there comes a day when, with no second's warning, you are given the bleak message: "Son of man, behold I take away the desire of thine eyes at a stroke; yet neither shalt thou weep, nor let the tears run down...So I preached unto the people in the morning: and in the evening my wife died" (Ezek. 24:16, 18). Suppose that, to you, as to Christ, it became evident that life was not to give what you expected from it, that your dreams were not to be granted, that yours was to be a steep and lonely road, that some tremendous sacrifice was to be asked of you, could you adjust to face it with a shadow of the Master's courage and the Master's calm? For there is no supposing in the matter. It is a certainty to you too, in your turn, someday, these things must come.

Trials Must Come

Yes, unbelievably they come. For years and years, you and I go our sunny ways and live our happy lives, and the rumors of these terrors are blown to us very faintly as from a world so distant that it seems to have nothing to do with us; and then, to us, too, it happens. And when it does, nobody has the right to snivel or whimper as if something unique and inexplicable had befallen him. "Never morning wore to evening but some heart did break"—hearts just as sensitive as yours and mine. But when yours breaks, what then? It is a bit late in the day to be talking about insurance when one's house is ablaze from end to end; and somewhat tardy to be searching for something to bring one through when the test is upon one. And how are you and I, so constantly complaining and easily fretted by the minor worries, to cope at all in the swelling of the Jordan, with the cold of it catching away our breath, and the rush of it plucking at our footing?

Goethe, of course, tells us that all the religions were designed to meet us and to give us help, just there; to enable us to bear the unbearable, to face the impossible, to see through with some kind of decency and honor what obviously cannot be done at all.

But, then, so many people's religion is a fair-weather affair. A little rain, and it runs and crumbles; a touch of strain, and it snaps. How often out at the battlefront one lay and watched an airplane high up in the blue and sunlight, a shimmering, glistening, beautiful thing; and then there came one shot out of a cloud, and it crashed down to earth, a broken mass of twisted metal. And many a one's religion is like that. So long as God's will runs parallel to ours, we follow blithely. But the moment that they cross or clash, that life grows difficult: that we do not understand, how apt faith is to fail us just when we have most need of it!

You remember our Lord's story of the two men who lived in the same village, went to the same synagogue and sat in the same pew, listening to the same services, and how one day, some kind of gale blew into their lives, a fearsome storm. And in the one case, everything collapsed, and for a moment there were some poor spars tossing upon wild waters, and then, nothing at all. For that unhappy soul had built on sand, and in his day of need, everything was undermined and vanished. But the other, though he, too, had to face the emptiness, the loneliness, the pain, came through it all braver and stronger and mellower and nearer God. For he had built upon the rock. Well, what of you and me? We have found it a business to march with the infantry, how will we keep up with the horsemen; if the small ills of life have frayed our faith and temper, what will we do in the roar and the black swirl of Jordan?

That has always been my chief difficulty about preaching. Thomas Carlyle, you recall, used to say that the chirpy optimism of Emerson maddened him; Emerson across whose sheltered life no cloud or shadow was allowed to blow. He seemed to me, panted the other, like a man, standing himself well back out of the least touch of the spray, who throws chatty observations on the beauty of the weather to a poor soul battling for his life in huge billows that are buffeting the breath and the life out of him, wrestling with mighty currents that keep sweeping him away. It did not help.

And I, too, have had a happy life; and always when I have spoken of the Gospel, and the love of God, and Christ's brave reading of this puzzling life of ours, it has seemed to me that a very easy answer lay ready to anybody's hand who found these hard to credit. Yes, yes, they might well say irritably, if I stood in the sunshine where you are, no doubt I, too, could talk like that! But if your path ran over the cold moors, where the winds cut and whistle and pierce to the very bone, if you were sat down where I am, I wonder if you would be so absolutely sure? As William Shakespeare says, it is not difficult to bear other people's toothache; but when one's own jaw is throbbing, that is another matter. We will listen to Jesus Christ—for He spoke from the darkness round the Cross. We may not understand Him, or agree with Him, or obey Him, but nobody can challenge His right to speak. But you! Wait until you stand in the rushing of the Jordan, to you there has come some fulfilment of that eerie promise, "Behold, your house is left unto you desolate," (Matt: 23:38). And what will you say then?

The Test of Faith

I will tell you now. I know that we are warned in Job that the most drastic test of faith is not even these tremendous sorrows, but a long purgatory of physical and mental agony. Still, I do not think that any one will challenge my right to speak today. And what I have to say is this: when Claverhouse suddenly shot Brown of Priesthill, the callous brute turned to the wife and asked, "What think you now of your fine teacher." And she, gathering together the scattered brain, answered "I always thought greatly of him, but I think more of him now." I always thought greatly of the Christian faith; but I think more of it now, far more. I have never claimed to understand many things in this perplexing life of ours, have always held that my dear master Browning went much too far when he said confidently that for a Christian man there are no problems in the world or out of it.

Surely, that acknowledgement of God's love raises new problems. If love, then why and why and why and why? To me, the essence of the faith has always seemed a certain intrepidity of loyalty that can believe undauntedly in the dark, and that still trusts God unshaken even when the evidence looks fairly damning. Do you think Christ always understood or found it easy? There was a day when He took God's will for Him into His hand, turned it round, and looked at it: "Is this what You ask of Me?" He said; and for a moment His eyes looked almost incredulous. Yes, and another day when puzzled and uncertain, He cried out, "But is this really what You mean that I should give You, this here, this now?" Yes, and another still, when the cold rushing waters roared in a raging torrent through His soul, yet He would not turn back, fought His way to the farther bank and died, still believing in the God who seemed to have deserted Him. That is why He is given a name that is above every name.

I do not understand this life of ours; but still less can I comprehend how people in trouble and loss and bereavement can run away peevishly from the Christian faith. In God's name, run to what? Have we not lost enough without losing that too? If Christ is right—if, as He says, there are somehow, hidden away from our eyes as yet, still there, wisdom and planning and kindness and love in these dark dispensations—then we can see them through. But if Christ was wrong, and all that is not so; if God set His foot on my home crudely, heedlessly, blunderingly, blindly, as I unexpectedly might tread upon some insect in my path, have I not the right to be angry and sore? If Christ was right, and immortality and the dear hopes of which He speaks do really lie a little way ahead, we can manage to make our way to them. But if it is not so, if it is all over, if there is nothing more, how dark the darkness grows! You people in the sunshine may believe the faith, but we in the shadow must believe it. We have nothing else!

Further, there is a grave saying in Scripture, "Receive not the grace of God in vain" (2 Cor. 6:1). That Christ should die on our behalf, that God should lavish His kindness on us, and that nothing should come of it, how terrible! And is it not pitiful if we receive the discipline of life in vain: have all the suffering of it, pay down the price in full, yet miss what it was sent to teach! I know that at first great sorrow is just stunned, that the sore heart is too numbed to feel anything, even God's hand.

When his wife died, Rossetti tells us, he passed through all that tremendous time with a mind absolutely blank, learned nothing, saw nothing, felt nothing; so that, looking back, all he could say was that, sitting in the forest with his head in his hands, somehow it was photographed permanently on his passive mind that a certain wild flower has three petals. That was all. But, by and by, the gale dies down, the moon rises, and throws a lane of gold to us across the blackness and the heaving of the tumbling waters. After all, it is not in the day, but in the night, that star rises after star, constellation follows constellation, and the immensity of this bewildering universe looms up before our staggered minds. And it is in the dark that the faith becomes biggest and bravest, that its wonder grows yet more and more. "Grace," said Samuel Rutherford, "grows best in the winter." And already some things have become very clear to me.

Faith Is Real

This to begin, that the faith works, fulfils itself, is real; and that its most audacious promises are true. Always we must try to remember that the glorious assertions of the Scriptures are not mere suppositions and guesses. There is no perhaps about them. These splendid truths are flowers that human hands like ours plucked in the gardens of their actual experience. Why is the prophet so sure that, as one whom his mother comforts, so will God comfort all hurt things? How did the Psalmist know that, those who are broken in their hearts and grieved in their minds, God heals? Because, of course, it had happened to them; because they had themselves in their dark days felt His unfailing helpfulness and tenderness and the touch of wonderfully gentle hands. And it is true.

When we are cast into some burning, fiery furnace seven times heated, we are not alone, never alone; but there is One beside us, like unto the Son of God. When our feet slip upon the slimy stones in the swelling of Jordan, a hand leaps out and catches us and steadies us. "I will not leave you comfortless," said Christ, Nor does He! There is a Presence with us, a Comforter, a Fortifier, who strengthens, upholds and brings us through somehow from hour to hour and day to day.

Pusey once wrote that when his wife died, he felt "as if the rushing waters were up to my chin; but underneath the chin there is a hand, supporting it." And that hand is there. As the days go by, what grows upon one more and more is the amazing tenderness of God. "Like as a father pitieth his children" (Ps. 103:13), mused a psalmist long ago. I have been wondering these days whether he, too, poor soul, suddenly, without one second's warning, had to tell his children that their mother was dead, and that remembrance of that agony made him sure, all his days, that it is not willingly that God afflicts and grieves us children of men. Anyhow that is true.

There is a marvellous picture in the National Gallery. Christ hangs upon the cross in a dense darkness; and, at first, that is all one sees. But, as one peers into the background, gradually there stands out another form, God's form; and other hands supporting Christ, God's hands; and another face, God's face, more full of agony even than our Savior's own. The presence, the sufficiency, the sympathy of God, these things grow very real and very sure and very wonderful!

The Certainty of Immortality

Further, *one becomes certain about immortality*. You think that you believe in that. But wait till you have lowered your dearest into an open grave, and you will know what believing it means. I have always gazed up at Paul in staggered admiration when he burst out at the grave's mouth into his scornful challenge, his exultant ridicule of it, "O death, where is thy sting? O grave, where is thy victory?" (1 Cor. 15:55). But now it does not seem to me such a tremendous feat—for I have felt that very same. True, I can tell him where death's sting lies. Ah! it is the constant missing of what used to be always here; the bitter grudging every second of the dear body to the senseless earth; the terrible insecurity, for one is never safe—anything, nothing, and the old overwhelming pain comes rushing back. Yet, when the other day I read a magazine, it was with amazement I discovered they are still chattering about whether we people are immortal or not. I am past that. I know! "I believe in the communion of saints, the forgiveness of sins, the resurrection of the body, and the life everlasting."

Unchristian Thoughts About Death

But, there is one thing I should like to say which I have never dared to say before, not feeling that I had the right. We Christian people as a whole are entirely unchristian in our thoughts of death. We have our eyes wrongly focused. We are selfish, self-centered, and self-absorbed. We keep thinking aggrievedly of what it means to us; and that is wrong, all wrong!

In the New Testament, you hear very little of the families with that aching gap, huddled together in their desolate little home in some back street; but a great deal about the saints in glory, and the sunshine, and the singing, and the splendor yonder. And, surely, that is where our thoughts should dwell. I, for one, want no melancholious tunes, no grey and sobbing words, but brave hymns telling of their victory. Dante had a sour mind. Yet, as he went up the hill that cleanses him that climbs, suddenly it shook and reeled beneath him. "What's that?," he cried out in alarm. And his guide smiled. "Some happy soul," he said, "has burst through into victory and every other on the mount is so praising God for that, that the whole hill rocks and staggers." And is not that the mood that best becomes us? Think about your brooding. What exactly does it mean? Would you pluck the diadem from their brows again? Would you snatch the palms of victory out of their hands? Dare you compare the clumsy nothings our poor blundering love can give them here with what they must have yonder where Christ Himself has met them, and has heaped on them, who can but fathom, what happiness and glory? I love to picture it. How, shyly, amazed, half protesting, she who never thought of self was led into the splendor of her glory. As the old poet put it centuries ago,

> Our sweet is mixed with bitter gall,
>   Our pleasure is but pain,
> Our joys scarce last the looking on,
>   Our sorrows still remain.
>
> But there they have such rare delights,
>   Such pleasure and such play,
> That unto them a thousand years
>   Doth seem but yesterday.

To us, it will be long and lonesome; but they will not even have looked round them before we burst in. In any case, are we to let our dearest be wrenched out of hands by force? Or, seeing that it has to be, will we not give them willingly and proudly, looking God in the eyes, and telling Him that we prefer our loneliness rather than that they should miss one tittle of their rights. When the blow fell, that was the one and only thought that kept beating like a hammer in my brain. I felt I had lost her forever, must have lost her; that to all eternity she must shine far ahead of me; and my heart kept crying out, "I choose it, I choose it, do not for my sake deny her anything." I know, now, that I have not lost her. For love is not a passing thing one leaves behind. And is it not love's way to stoop? When we are young, we think of heaven as a vague, nebulous, and shadowy place. But as our friends gather there, more and more it gains body, vividness, and homeliness. And when our dearest have passed yonder, how real and evident it grows, how near it: "Where our treasure is, there will our heart be also," (Matt: 6:21; Luke 12:34). Never again will I give out that stupid lie, "There is a happy land, far, far away." It is not far. They are quite near. And the communion of the saints is a tremendous and most blessed fact.

I do not think you need to be afraid of life. Our hearts are very frail; and there are places where the road is very steep and very lonely. But we have a wonderful God. And as Paul puts it in Romans 8:35, what can separate us from His love? Not death, he says immediately, pushing that aside at once as the most obvious of all impossibilities.

No, not death, For, standing in the roaring of the Jordan, cold to the heart with its dreadful chill, and very conscious of the terror of its rushing, I, too, like Hopeful, can call back to you who, one day in your turn, will have to cross it, "Be of good cheer, my brother, for I feel the bottom, and it is sound."

NOTES

Changes of Life and Their Comforts in God

John Ker (1819-1886) is little known today, but in his day he was a respected preacher and professor of preaching and pastoral work at the United Free Church Seminary in Glasgow, Scotland. He published two volumes of sermons: this one is from the *Sermons First Series,* published in Edinburgh in 1870 by Edmonston and Douglas.

John Ker

2

CHANGES OF LIFE
AND THEIR COMFORTS IN GOD

Yet the Lord will command his loving kindness in the daytime, and in the night his song shall be with me, and my prayer unto the God of my life (Psalm 42:8).

PSALMS 42 AND 43 have so close a connection that they must be regarded as one. The same struggle and victory pass through them, and they are necessary to complete each other. From external and internal evidence, they belong to David and to that part of his life when he was fleeing from the face of Absalom his son.

All must recollect the touching scene when he left his palace, crossed the brook Kidron, "went up by the ascent of Mount Olivet, and wept as he went up, and had his head covered; and he went barefoot: and all the people that were with him covered every man his head, and they went up, weeping as they went" (2 Sam. 15:30). He was not so great in his youth, crowned with Goliath's trophies, nor in manhood, when God delivered him from the hand of Saul and set him on the throne of Israel, as in that hour of desertion. It is then that the character comes forth, that faith flames high, and the feet find their rock in God. When we can look back on our own lives, as we now do on David's, we shall perceive that such times have been, not the depths, but the heights of the soul.

It is here that we can look into the heart of David and know how, in some measure, he was according to the heart of God. When the priests would have borne the ark with him into exile, the noble magnanimity, the deep submission of his spirit, is seen. "Carry back the ark of God," he said, "into the city; if I shall find favor in the eyes of the Lord, He will bring me again, and show me both it and His habitation. But if He thus say, I have no delight in thee; behold, here am I, let Him do to me as seemeth good unto Him!" (2 Sam. 15:25, 26). By one of those strange circles of events, which have surely in them a Divine plan, he was treading the very soil of Gethsemane, and up through his heart there was throbbing the spiritual life of his Son and Lord, "Not my will, but thine be done."

It was not indifference to the ark of God that prompted the word of David. Banished beyond Jordan, among the forests and cataracts of the mountain land of Gilead, where "deep calling to deep," in the torrents around him, seemed emblems of his trials, his heart turns to the hallowed spot—"true as the dial to the sun, although it be not shone upon." It breaks out in every part of this song. The first verse is a longing wish after it, the last a joyful conviction that he shall reach it. Three times his soul is cast down in him, and three times he rises stronger for his fall, the onset of his faith ending like the apostle Paul's, "for this I besought the Lord thrice," and, like that of a greater still, who "prayed thrice, using the same words."

The verse we have selected is from one of the seasons of comfort. In the third verse he had said, "My tears have been my meat day and night, while they continually say unto me, Where is thy God?" Day and night God's hand was heavy upon him, so that "his moisture was turned into the drought of summer," and now he feels that day and night God's comforts can be with him. It is wonderful when we open these ancient books to find the identity of human life. As men speak, we can feel the beatings of the same heart and see the tears upon their face which make us children of one family. We can see, not less, the identity of the life that is divine—for God's light is shining down into their souls and making them strong with the strength of the Eternal. It is to make us feel this that we have such a Bible, and it is thus we must seek to use it.

Must Be Changes in Every Life

The *first* thought we would draw from this verse is that

there must be changes in every true life. These changes give
to life the *most opposed conditions*—light and darkness.

There is day, and there is night. That these are, in the
first place, to be taken literally is admitted, and that we
are taught to look to an unchanging God through all the
changes of natural time. But that day and night look further than this is seen from the whole tenor of the psalm
and from the usage of Scripture language. They represent the shiftings of color which pass across our history,
from the broad bright sunshine of prosperity to the
darkest and heaviest of our trials. If our life is to be of
any value, these must come in some form, outwardly or
inwardly. "Because they have no changes," says the
Psalmist, "therefore they fear not God" (Ps. 55:19). To
be convinced of this, we have only to look at the lives of
those who have come forth as strong, true men on God's
side; at the vicissitudes in the course of Abraham, and
Jacob, and Moses, and David; at the conflicts of the
followers of Christ; above all, at the life of the Great Head
Himself.

What a breadth of experience there was in Christ! First,
the day of brightness which He left, then what may be
called his night season in this world, and now again His
exceeding gladness in the light of God. His earthly life,
set like a night between these two great days, had also
its changes. He had His time for the transfiguration robes,
and His cry up through the darkness of the cross; His
moments when He rejoiced in spirit, "I thank Thee, O
Father," and His hours of sorrow even unto death. A
broad experience like this runs, more or less, through the
history of all who belong to Him. The more we study their
lives and seek to enter into sympathy with them, the more
we shall feel that our life cannot be uniform and that,
above all, we must be made partakers of the suffering.
Shall we repine when God puts us among the children
and makes us conformable to Christ? If we have the sharp
and sudden fall, as over a precipice, we hear some of them
saying, "Thou hast lifted me up and cast me down;" and
if we have weary, wistful looks on through a life, where
all seems darkened and the sweet of existence crushed

out forever, another says, "I shall go softly all my years, in the bitterness of my soul." There is no place so gloomy, where we cannot see the trace of some foot, now "standing in God's even place," nor so lonely, where Christ has not been and (shall we not say?) where Christ is now. Let us settle it with ourselves that such changes must come to us, and let this give us, I do not say submission but acquiescence. It is the lot of the family—it is more—it is the life of Christ, and it must be spread throughout the members.

These changes, let it be observed, are *according to a fixed law*. Day and night are the ordinances of heaven upon earth for the growth of earth's life, and, if we could trace the sunshine and the dark in every follower of God, we should see them arranged with equal wisdom. It is a more complex work, but, be sure of this, there is order in it all, and the hand that rules the world in its orbit, and that makes it fulfill its course through light and shade, is governing our lives for a higher than earthly end.

One feature of the law is presented so far for our guidance. *It is a law of alternation.* These changes give place to each other in succession. It is day and night, and, let us thank God, it is also in due time night and day. Each has its time and use.

In general, *God sends to us a portion of the day before the night.* There are, in the natural life, happy homes of childhood; loving hearts so close to us, that they shut out all evil beyond; fond fancies and bright hopes which make an Eden begin our memory, as it does the world's. The Christian life is even so. It is usually, at first, a simple, humble apprehension of God's mercy which gives the love of youth and knows not the pains of backsliding, nor the chillness of decline. It is in kindness that God begins our life with such a day-time. It strengthens us for the trial and creates a memory within, which can be nourished into a hope. It helps us all to reason with the ancient patriarch Job, "Shall we receive good at the hand of God, and shall we not receive evil?" (Job 2:10). If we have had our day, it is our duty and our strength not to forget it. The great poet, who said that "nothing can be more wretched than to remember happiness in misery," was surely wrong. To remember what is truly good is to possess it forever.

But after day it is God's manner sooner or later to send night. It is night that lets us measure the day. The daylight cannot be estimated when we are in it. It needs night to look back on it, to see what is true and false, what is solid and empty. At night we can tell our work and count our gains and resolve, if another day be granted, that tomorrow shall not be as this day, but much more abundant. It is night that lets us measure ourselves. We cannot know self by day. We are mixed with the busy distracting world, dispersed and confused in action and enjoyment. The night comes to let the thoughts concentrate and fall back on their real strength, to make them feel what basis they have within: "Thou hast proved my heart, Thou hast visited me in the night" (Psalm 17:3). It is night that lets us measure the real universe. By day, it is shut. We see only this earth and earthly sun. By night, God withdraws the veil, reveals eternity with its far-off shores of sparkling worlds, and fills the soul with infinite longings, which make it conscious it has a universe within greater than the universe without, and which can be satisfied only with God. It learns to stretch its arms up to that world where there shall be no more night and to Him who fills it: "O that I knew where I might find Him, that I might come even to his seat."

For these, and many other ends, does God let night fall upon the soul. If day has its light and its gladness and its walk and its work, night has its sense of void, better than earth's fulness, and its deep thoughts and humble waiting and sighing aspirations for the dawn—its refreshing dew below, its far beacon lights of stars above, which are nearer eternity than the sun's brightness.

And yet we cannot wish that God should close our view of this life with night. It is a true feeling which is expressed by the ancient mourner, "I had fainted unless I had believed to see the goodness of the Lord in the land of the living." We long to have the night break up before we die, to have some horizon-streak of the coming day, which may make the word true, "it shall come to pass that at evening-time it shall be light"—a glimpse of dawn like Simeon's view, or Stephen's, or the calm that fell on Christ's own struggle before He died. There is a light indeed that vanishes from our life, which we feel can never come back—never here; "the tender grace of a day that is dead" is fled to the eternal shore, and our hearts would break to think that anything in this world's future could make us forget it or fill the blank.

But there is another kind of day which can come to the bitterness of utter bereavement. The Sun of Righteousness rises with healing. Our dead are given back to us in our souls, with more than the tenderness of life, and without the cruel pang of death. When we can hold them in our hearts without pain, we have recovered them. They ascend, as the Lord did, and sit in our thoughts in heavenly places with Him, calm and bright, and the tender grace of a bygone day puts on also the glory of a day to come. That such a day-spring even here can visit the darkest gloom of trial, let not any mourner doubt, who believes that Christ has left his own grave empty and that He will come to open ours. He can raise our friends from the bitterness of death and give them back to our spirits in this world, to speak and live, and even rejoice with them, that He may thus assure us He Himself is risen, and that they too shall yet be ours in full possession.

And, when such a day comes, it is to console the night—to make us feel that Christ's word, "Weep not," has power with the living before He touches the bier where the dead lie. Were He to suffer the cloud to hang forever as heavy and as dark, it would overwhelm us and misrepresent Him—"The spirit would fail before Him, and the souls that He has made." Such a day comes also to test the night, to try its thoughts and its resolves, if they are streadfast to their end, and, after testing, to mature them. In the hours of darkness the roots strike down, and the dew lies all night long on the branches, but the blossoms and the fruit demand the sun; and hope, love, higher fellowship with God, and deeper sympathy for suffering humanity, come forth afterward as the peaceable fruits of righteousness.

Divine Provisions for Changes in Life

The *second* thought contained in this passage is that *to suit these changes in life there are divine provisions.*

For the day, God commands "His loving-kindness"; for the night, He gives "His song." There must be something suitable in each of these provisions to the circumstances—the more so, that similar expressions are found in other passages of Scripture. The "songs of the night" is as favorite a word of the Old Testament as "glory in tribulation" is of the New, and it is one of those which prove that both Testaments have the self-same root and spirit.

The loving-kindness of God is a movement—not so much from us to God as from God to us—of which a believing man is not insensible, but toward which his position is more that of a passive recipient. It is God's goodness, like the daylight's gladness, thrown on and around him to lighten up his life. It is a promise which, to a thoughtful man, is very precious. Prosperity without God's favor in it is less than nothing; but if God's loving-kindness be there, it is better than life. It brings with it the assurance that all things work together for good to the man.

It secures this, in the beginning, that man shall have strength for every day's duty. There will be light to guide him in all his walk and grace to help him in all his work. It secures, next, that prosperity shall not injure him— "the sun shall not smite him by day" (Ps. 121:6). If it be God's gentleness which has made him great, that gentleness shall dwell also within and make him able to say, "Lord, my heart is not haughty, nor mine eyes lofty" (Ps. 131:1); and that times may come when a man must take up such language in the sight of God against accusers, no one who reads the words of Job or David or Paul, not to speak of Christ himself, can doubt.

This loving-kindness secures, still further, that prosperity shall have its true enjoyment. God's love gives to a man the very life of life and bestows on the day that light of which the poet speaks—"a brighter light than ever shone on sea or shore." Every blessing, every happy affection, every tender touch of kindred souls, is a drop from the river of life and a foretaste of the fountain-head. If we possess it, let us be glad, and, if we have lost it, let us still be glad, for the gifts and calling of God are without repentance. These, too, like our friends, are not lost, but gone before. There are some who tremble when they look back on past hours of joy and bear contrition for their too great happiness, as Job sacrificed for his sons when they feasted; but if God's loving kindness was there, the daylight was good and pure, and it has done its part. It has strengthened the heart for trial, filled it with happy memories, and given it power to cherish happier hopes. If we are children of the light and of the day, we need retain no fear, because we have had our heart made joyful by the Father of lights.

It might seem as if there were nothing better than this, a day in which "God commands his loving-kindness;" and yet, the order in which this stands, and the whole spirit of the Bible, teach us to look for something higher in night when "He gives His song." The loving-kindness is God's goodness *on* and *around* us, the song His goodness *in* and passing *through* us. The song is the realizing of the loving-kindness—the light that shines around, entering into the soul as night deepens and giving day in its center. It is the pillar of cloud kindling up into the pillar of fire.

Those to whom God draws near in an agony of grief understand this. If there are hours in our life when we know that there is a living God and an eternal world, it is in such a crisis, when we are compelled to cling to Him in the dark and feel, as we cling, a strength beneath that lifts us up. This could never be, if there were not a God, and, I can suppose, that Christ may permit death to enter a home, and delay His deliverance, that He may bring us to this issue. Who knows whether at Bethany a greater work was not done in the house of mourning, than outside at the grave? It is then that God enters and heaven opens, and that we know what it is to have strength in weakness, and peace in trouble, and to bear a crushing load, and to feel One bearing us. This is God's way of help, so good for us, so glorifying to Himself; and whenever it comes, in whatever degree, it is "His song in the night."

The song in the night is not only this conscious feeling, it is the expression of it—to ourselves and others. It may not be loud—not even whispered in words—but it is a resignation to the will of God, that is calm and sweet, that speaks often loudest when the lips are dumb, and lets itself be known by its perfume, like a flower in the dark.

Where there is song, there is the token of freedom from terror. God's own voice has hushed the soul, "Fear not, for I am with thee," till it replies, "I will fear no evil, for Thou art with me" (Ps. 23:4). The song tells of a coming end to darkness, for there is prophecy in it, and wherever there is this deepest harmony—the heart at one with God in sorrow,—the highest hope is never far away. It comes like those faithful women to the sepulchre, in the morning while it is yet dark, and finds, to its wonder, a risen Lord.

If you search the history of God's dealings, you will find that it has been His manner to give these songs in the deepest night to those who look to Him. In the time of Job. He was known as "God our maker, who giveth songs in the night" (Job 35:10). Asaph remembered his "song in the night, when he communed with his heart" (Ps. 77:6); and what are David's psalms in trouble, but songs when God made "the very night to be light about him"? Paul and Silas found it in prison, when "they prayed and sang praises at midnight, and the prisoners heard them" (Acts 16:25), for He in whom they trusted made his comforts come gliding like his own angels, through the prison bars, till strange sounds of song, such as dungeons had not known before, came floating to the wondering listeners. In privation, in bereavement, in desertion, in death, these utterances of confidence in God are written down for us. In the night of trial, He has filled the history of His church as full of songs beneath, as there are stars of promise above. They console the hearts of the singers, and they rise to join the songs of the morning stars—to announce that a ransomed company is marching through the gloom, anticipating the time when they too "shall obtain joy and gladness, and sorrow and sighing shall flee away."

Means for Change in Life

The *third* and last thought is that *there is a constant duty on our part amid all.*

"And my prayer unto the God of my life!" If we are to be safe in these changes and to share these Divine provisions, here are the means: "Life"—someone has said—"is a constant want, therefore it should be a constant prayer." It is not that we are to sublimate this duty into one unvaried feeling and to withdraw it from every act of time and place; for those who do so must be more than common men, if prayer, as a feeling, does not soon drop and die. The day and the night call upon us to sanctify each, by its own form, to God, and some days and nights in their temptations and sorrows demand those wrestlings that have power with God to prevail. Let us never forget that the Savior of the world found it needful so to cry to His Father, and that the world's redemption passed through its crisis in an act of special prayer. If our hours of sorrow lead to such outpourings of heart, we are on our way to the songs of the night. To pray truly, is to praise. Therefore, in such supreme moments of our being, let us "stir ourselves up to take hold of God."

But neither are we to confine the prayer within such limits. Those who are most earnest and deep at central points will spread most widely the feeling of prayer all through time. The throb of the heart will pulsate to the extremity, and prayer will be like the movement of life, which beats so constantly, because it is a dying and reviving in every pulse-stroke. The essence of this feeling is dependence upon God. It is a dependence that is reverent and yet loving, reasonable and yet childlike, that is not inconsistent with action, no, that is impious and vain unless it is breathing its life into every fitting duty. It will put the question, "What wilt Thou have me to do?" and be ready to work by day or watch by night, as He may give the word. "Lord teach us so to pray!"

It is to the "God of our life." The God, is it not, of *all our life, of every day and night—who orders them and bids them come and go, as He orders light and darkness to flicker over the face of the earth? To Him we pray, for "all our times are in his hand." It is to the God of the great movements* of our life. When all the joy, or, still more, all the agony, is gathered into one cup, and we are bidden to drink; and He is seen to hold it in His hand, what can we do but pray to Him then? "God of my life, to Thee I call." It is to the God of our *eternal* life, and bitter without any sweet that cup would be and cruel the hand that pressed it to our lips, if we could not add this—*God of our eternal life!* It is this that more than accounts for the agony, and this that summons to unfailing prayer. For, apart from the promises of his own Word and the revelation of Jesus Christ, we may argue, that the God who sends such agony on human hearts must have a great purpose beyond, which will justify Him before His universe, and that the God who admits a creature to speak to Him and gives comfort and joy in the thought of his own fellowship, cannot remand that creature to everlasting forgetfulness. Here, suffering and prayer meet and clasp hands around eternal life and Him who is the God of it.

We can't help but think that these men of old, who so wrestled with sorrow, in the power of prayer, had that faith which made them feel, that death is not an eternal farewell to God. It is surely the first instinct of life to cling to its own preservation, and shall this not be true of the life which is Divine? And we, who have a clearer light, or rather life brought to light, shall we not feel it more? *My prayer to the God of my eternal life!* In such times, our prayer should be that He, who is proving Himself a Father to our spirits, may make this highest life His care and ours, that the rending of our dearest earthly affections may bind us closer to Him who can heal them again, and that, over the graves of our lost and longed for, we may have a firmer hold of that God who is "the God not of the dead, but of the living."

If happiness be the end of life, as some would tell us, life in this world is a great and manifest failure. But, if it be something more—if it be to train the soul in reverence, faith, and obedience to God—then, with much that is dark, we have some light on our way through the terrible mysteries which surround us. Let us pursue our way with this guide, "my prayer to the God of my life"—humbly trusting in, and following Him who struggled in the deepest darkness for us. Be sure that they who follow Him must come to the light of life. If we have, meanwhile, day, we shall have that loving-kindness which makes it doubly bright; and in the deepest night, we shall not be hopeless, but we shall cherish that "song in the night" which comes as "when a holy solemnity is kept" (Is. 30:29)—a deep resignation to the supreme will that waits for the morning, which must come as sure as there is a God—and for melodies, which shall not be low in the heart, but loud and joyful on the tongue, for "those that dwell in the dust shall awake and sing."

NOTES

Christ in a World of Pain

William M. Clow (1853-1930) was born in
Scotland and educated in Auckland, New
Zealand, and Glasgow. From 1881 to 1911, he
pastored five churches in Scotland, and then
joined the faculty of the United Free Church
College in Glasgow. He taught theology for
several years and closed his ministry as prin-
cipal of the college. *The Cross in Christian
Experience* and *The Day of the Cross* are two
of his most popular books. This sermon comes
from *The Secret of the Lord* which was
published in 1911 in London by Hodder and
Stoughton.

William M. Clow

3

CHRIST IN A WORLD OF PAIN

And when they were come to the multitude, there came to Him a certain man, kneeling down to Him, and saying, Lord, have mercy on my son (Matthew 17:14).

YOU ARE FAMILIAR with Raphael's glowing conception of the Transfiguration of Christ. He has daringly painted two pictures in a single space. In the upper half of the picture we see Christ with His shining face and His glistering garments, while Moses and Elias pay Him homage, and Peter and James and John fall prostrate at His feet. In the lower part of the picture we are shown the scene at the foot of the mountain—the baffled disciples, the mocking scribes, the pressing and staring multitude—and, in the foreground, the anguished father with his epileptic child. The painter's purpose is to emphasize that strange contrast, so often seen in Christ's experience, between the hours of spiritual rapture and the hours of struggle with strife and care and sorrow of life. In a single glance we see the ineffable splendor and serene felicity of the mountaintop, and the misery and tears of the busy ways of men.

But this thought of the contrast between the heavenly peace of the mountain-top and the fretting and discord and burden at its foot, so fascinating to art and so appealing to our own experience, is not the thought of the evangelists. They see not a contrast, but a sequence. It is to them a sequence as natural as noontide is to dawn, as the day of toil is to the quiet night of rest. They show us Jesus coming down from His transfiguring hour with the secret of His cross locked in His heart. They record the quiet talk by the way. They bid us mark Him entering into the midst of the excited multitude. But His state is kingly still. It is the same Jesus, whose face was illumined by the light from within, passing on, to stand in the midst of the strife and pain of the world.

There are two transfigurations. There is the transfiguration in prayer, when the soul sends its flush in illumining power to the brow. There is the transfiguration in service, when all the tender and self-denying emotions of the heart flood the face with love light. We see the one in the transfiguration of the mother who prays for her little child. The other transfiguration was seen by the men who lay on their sleepless beds of pain in the hospital of Scutari, when Florence Nightingale passed with her lamp through their wards in the night watches, ministering to their needs. Against the dark background of human pain; these evangelists see the glory of Christ as clearly as in the light of the open heaven. They see Christ coming to the multitude and proving Himself the Master of its pain.

When we read the story of this epileptic and devil-possessed child, we find that we are reading an epitome of the pain of humility. There is the torture of the writhing body and the disorder of the mind whose sweet reason is overthrown. There is the spectacle of a soul held and driven by the dominion of evil. There is the shadowed home of the child, with those long years of broken-hearted shame and agonizing exposure. There is the despairing father, loving his child the more tenderly for his affliction, and wounded in the marrow of his heart. There is the wonder and crude pity and bewildered questioning of the multitude. There are the baffled would-be healers of the distraught boy. All that can be packed into the word pain, of torture, and anguish, and perplexity is summed up in this graphic picture of the gnashing child and the father's tears and the multitude's wondering sorrow. Let us see how Christ bears Himself in a world of pain.

Christ's Keen Consciousness of Pain

The world was very beautiful to Jesus. He entered with zest into the glory of earth and sea and sky. The rich, green flush of the meadows caught His eyes with a swift thrill of joy, and He saw the lilies spreading the earth with scarlet. He marked the sparrows building in the

eaves. He had stood silent as He watched the coming of
the dawn and looked into the splendor of the setting sun.
Home, love, friendship made Him glad. But through it
all, He heard the cry of pain, now low, moaning, and
hopeless, and again wailing and shrieking in agony.

A master of music will hear and be tortured by a single
insistent discord. A compassionate heart will pass by the
stately buildings of a great city when his eyes have been
caught by the misery of its poor. A traveller in Central
Africa will be withdrawn from the marvels of lake and
river, of forest and swamp, when he sees the white trail
of bleaching bones which marks the slave trader's track.
So, Jesus moved in this world of beauty and light with
a keen consciousness of pain. He never came to a
multitude without being touched by its sorrow. His por-
trait, as He looks out on any crowd of men, has been
drawn for us in a single line: "Jesus, moved with compassion." Here He comes to this multitude, marks the
surging of the crowd, sees the taunting scribes, looks with
vexation and weariness on His powerless and downcast
disciples, and He has His keen consciousness of pain. But,
when the father brings his child to Him all else is forgotten. With eyes soft with pity, in gentle question, and with
keen appeal, He bends Himself to the healing of the child.

Christ moved in a world of sorrow. He saw the leper by
the wayside and never ceased to bear his disease. He heard
the cry of the blind when others passed them by. He felt
the touch of the woman in the thronging crowd. He stood
up to gaze upon the man, blind from his birth, at the door
of the temple with a sigh in His heart. He marked the
widow weeping by her son's bier. He saw the hungering,
wistful, wandering crowd as sheep without a shepherd.
He looked upon a city hastening all unaware to its doom
and was moved to tears. He saw not merely the pain and
the sorrow which all men's eyes might have marked. He
saw into the depths of men's souls, away behind their
callous faces and high looks and stoical pose. He saw how
surely the bravest and proudest come to the hour of agony,
and how universal is the crown of sorrow. Never did
morning wear to evening but Christ's heart did break.

Christ's Acceptance of Pain

To see Jesus moving in the midst of a world of pain, keenly conscious of it and yet forbearing to heal, is, at first sight, both a marvel and a mystery. There were many widows in Israel who mourned for their children, but the Son of man did not regard Himself as sent to them. There were many lepers who prayed for cleansing, but Christ did not heal them. There were more sisters than Martha and Mary who wept beside their brother's grave, but Christ had no word for them. There were lame and crippled and blind in every village through which Jesus passed, but they were lame and crippled and blind to the last chapter of their lives.

The mystery of pain which burdens so many tender minds today is darkest when we think of Christ. We wonder why God permits so much suffering. We grow chill in heart when we recall our unanswered prayers. We almost revolt when we see that the noblest and gentlest and bravest spend so many years of anguish. When we stop to listen to the cries of neglected and piteously wronged children, to the sobs of fear and loneliness and bereavement, to the muttered exclamations of tortured men crushed amid merciless machineries, to the groans of the wounded and dying on the field of battle, we wonder how God bears the burden of it. When we think of the silent and nameless sorrows of men and women who dare not tell us why they suffer, we cry, "My God, my God, why—?" But Christ has no outcry at pain. He did ask, once, and once only, "My God, My God, why—?", but it was why God had forsaken Him, not why He suffered. To Christ there was neither marvel nor mystery in sorrow. He was marked by a quiet acceptance of pain.

Why Christ Accepted Pain

1. There are three reasons why Jesus accepted pain. The first is, that, in a world like ours, under the laws of a moral governor, and full of living creatures with exquisite and delicate nerves, and keen and tender senses, and hearts that can love and sorrow, *pain is inevitable.* Pain

is the swift and wise and necessary consequence of the breaking of God's law. Whenever, either in ignorance, or by accident, or by careless disobedience, or by gross and willful wrong-doing, God's law is broken, pain follows as closely and inescapably as a shadow. A wild beast treads carelessly, while he crouches for his prey, upon a thorn. The keen dart of pain tells him of his folly. A little child touches the glowing ribs of the grate. The instant burn is never forgotten. A man builds a wall with untempered mortar, or drives a rivet slackly home, or lights a match in a mine, and there is a harvest of agony of which he may never know. A man trifles once and once only with the law of self-restraint. Before the morning light he is touched by the wounding finger of pain. It could not be otherwise. Pain is the hedge by which God guards His narrow way. Pain is the angel with the drawn sword which keeps the way of the tree of life. Pain is the goad which compels men to a carefulness they would not take, and to toils they would not endure. The upward climb of the race, and its conquest of earth and sea and sky, with its constant advance in knowledge and power and skill, is greatly motived by pain. But for this sharp stroke of pain, men might sink back into the slime.

2. The second reason why Jesus accepted pain is that *He realized its beneficent office.* Pain is not only the angel with the drawn sword, but the prophet whose voice no man can neglect. There are some men and women who have had little pain. They have inherited superb physical strength, a comely beauty, and a full share of mental ability. They have ample wealth and high position in society. They have never known the feeling of want or had any anxiety about tomorrow's bread. Their minds are untroubled and their sleep is sweet. But these are never men and women of high and noble and tender spirit. They do not see visions nor dream dreams. Their voices are never tremulant with hope and joy in God. You must go to some poor stricken creature who has been long companied with pain to mark the wide horizon of patient thought, to hear the noble music of an enlightened heart, and to enter a world of which the coarse Philistine had

never dreamed. God could not work His will in us without this ministry of pain.

3. The third reason why Christ accepted pain *gives us a deeper insight into the mind of God.* Pain does not always chasten the sufferer. It sometimes hardens and embitters. It sometimes clouds the spirit and overthrows the mind. But there is one office it never fails to fulfil. It keeps men's hearts tender and pitiful and patient. If the world were full only of men and women who were all young and pulsing in health, self-sufficient in their strength, and unburdened in their thoughts, life would be almost intolerable. If there were no little children laid in their helplessness as burdens on our hearts, and no weak and old and ailing and helpless, and no sick and tortured, broken-hearted and dying, this world would be an arena in which the cruelest passions would rise in pitiless struggle. We have only to hear the cry of a lost child, or to enter a home where one lies long years on a bed of sickness wondering at God's strange ways, or to see a strong man smitten by some stroke which makes those who love him care for him with tender offices, to realize that pain with its solemn, unsmiling, and sometimes deeply-lined face, is a great servant of God. It has created our compassions, chastened our sympathies, purged us of our hardness and apathy and selfishness. It has wrought out in men a great part of the beauty of holiness. Christ saw this noble discipline on human character; and He accepted pain.

Christ's Deliverance From Pain

"They shall obtain joy and gladness, and sorrow and sighing shall flee away," sang the Old Testament prophet in Isaiah 35:10, and the New Testament poet makes his response, "And God shall wipe away all tears from their eyes; and there shall be no more death, neither sorrow nor crying, neither shall there by any more pain; for the former things are passed away" (Rev. 21:4). The day is coming when God shall no longer need the ministry of pain. But that day cannot come until all the causes of pain have been removed. Christ came not to cleanse the leper's scab, nor to make every lame man walk, nor to call back the dead from the grave, nor to wipe the tears from all the faces that He met. He would not have forgone His own hours of weeping. He came to deliver men from pain by quenching the bitter sources from which its streams issued. He came to redeem the world from that curse, of which pain is only one consequence.

> He comes to break oppression,
>   To set the captive free,
> To take away transgression,
>   And rule in equity.
> He comes with succor speedy
>   To those who suffer wrong,
> To help the poor and needy,
>   And bid the weak be strong.
> To give them songs for singing,
>   Their darkness turn to light
> Whose souls, condemned and dying,
>   Were precious in His sight.

He came to vanquish the wrong and to cancel the long inheritance of evil which lies behind all pain. When every wicked passion has been cast out, when men are living in a willing obedience to the law of God, when every wilful thought has been brought into captivity with Christ, when no prejudice can keep us back from knowing God's will, and no passion from doing it, then pain, which is but the sting of sin, shall be no more.

Notice Jesus, in the light of this ruling truth, dealing with this tormented child. What lay behind this writhing, and foaming and gnashing of teeth? What lies, either immediately or remotely, behind every torture that flesh or spirit have known. It is surely some spirit of evil. "Thou deaf and dumb spirit, I charge thee come out of him." When the spirit had departed, the pain had passed. That is how, then and always, Christ delivers from pain. When Christ has cast out from men's hearts the evil of greed, the sweating den, the mean street, the miserable home, the drink trade, the drug traffic, and all the wrongs which have so constant and so awful a consequence of pain, then shall all have passed away. When Christ has cast out the evil spirit of lust, the wrongs of womanhood, the curse of manhood, and the tell-tale marks on the bodies of little children, pain will no more be known. When Christ has cast out the evil spirit of ambition, there will be no tale of the victims of the war to count; and the widow and the orphan of the soldier will no longer be seen. When Christ casts out of men's heart's the evil spirit of gluttony and drunkenness, fewer women will weep, fewer men will be racked with disease, fewer babies will be born in shame, to live brief lives of weakness and misery. When Christ has cast out the evil spirit of pride and envy and jealousy, scorn will no longer make men bitter, and callous contempt no longer make them sad. Christ delivers from pain not by any anodyne; He robs it of its keenest edge, He quenches it by casting out the evil spirits who cause it.

Christ's Commission to His People of a Ministry to Pain

One of the first commands given by Christ was to heal the sick. It is plain that He expected that His disciples would have cast out this evil spirit. His reproach to them is the measure of the keenness of His disappointment at their failure. It reveals that the reason for their impotence was the ebbing of their faith. They could not cast the spirit out because they had lost the assurance and conviction that God was with them. That reproach of Christ smites us all. There are evils we could combat and overcome. There are wrongs we could redress. There are curses we could remove, if only we believed. The pain of the world could be lessened at least by one-half in a single week if only Christian men faced the ill-doing of our time in strength of self-denying faith. The Greathearts of our time who have freed the slave, rescued the lost, dried the widow's tears, and cared for the orphan, have all been men and women of invincible faith.

In his *Castles in the Air,* Stubbs tells the story of Miss Jones, the superintendent of the Liverpool Workhouse Hospital, who had heard of Christ's commission, and wrought out in her obedience the miracle of the healing of pain.

> A simple woman, weak, but strong in God,
> And Christ's great Gospel, told unto the poor,
> God's poor and dying on their pauper beds;
> Told not alone in wholesome words of good,
> But preached by tender hands upon the brow,
> And hovering tendance, calm and sweetly still.
>
> To many a foundering soul she stretched
> The hand of help: and from her eyes they caught
> The light of Heaven, that brightens into hope,
> The sinner's hope, from Him, the Crucified.

When Christ has such servants we shall have reached the eve of that day in which there shall be no more pain.

For the Troubled

Charles Haddon Spurgeon (1834-1892) is undoubtedly the most famous minister of modern times. Converted in 1850, he united with the Baptists and very soon began to preach in various places. He became pastor of the Baptist church in Waterbeach in 1851, and three years later he was called to the decaying Park Street Church, London. Within a short time, the work began to prosper, a new church was built and dedicated in 1861, and Spurgeon became London's most popular preacher. In 1855, he began to publish his sermons weekly; and today they make up the forty-nine volumes of *The Metropolitan Tabernacle Pulpit.* He founded a pastors' college and several orphanages. This sermon is taken from *The Metropolitan Tabernacle Pulpit,* volume XIX, published in 1874, and is from a sermon preached on January 12, 1873.

Charles H. Spurgeon

4

FOR THE TROUBLED

Thy wrath lieth hard upon me, and thou hast afflicted me with all thy waves (Psalm 88:7).

IT IS THE business of a shepherd not only to look after the happy ones among the sheep, but to seek after the sick of the flock and to lay himself out right earnestly for their comfort and succor. I feel, therefore, that I do rightly when I make it my special business to speak to such as are in trouble. Those of you who are happy and rejoicing in God, full of faith and assurance, can very well spare a discourse for your weaker brethren; you even can be glad and thankful to go without your portion in order that those who are depressed in spirit may receive a double measure of the wine of consolation.

It is clear to all those who read the narratives of Scripture, or are acquainted with good men, that the best of God's servants may be brought into the very lowest estate. There is no promise of present prosperity appointed to true religion, so as to exclude adversity from believers' lives. As men, the people of God share the common lot of men, and what is that but trouble? Yea, there are some sorrows which are peculiar to Christians, some extra griefs of which they partake because they are believers, though these are something more than balanced by those peculiar and bitter troubles, which belong to the ungodly and are engendered by their transgressions, from which the Christian is delivered.

From the passage which is open before us, we learn that sons of God may be brought so low as to write and sing psalms which are sorrowful throughout and have no fitting accompaniment but sighs and groans. They do not often do so; their songs are generally like those of David, which, if they begin in the dust, mount into the clear heavens before long; but sometimes, I say, saints are forced to sing such dolorous ditties, that from beginning to end there is not one note of joy. Yet, even in their dreariest winter night, the saints have an aurora in their sky; and in this eighty-eighth Psalm, the dreariest of all psalms, there is a faint gleam in the first verse, like a star-ray falling upon its threshold—"O Jehovah, God of my salvation." Heman retained his hold upon his God. It is not all darkness in a heart which can cry, "My God"; and the child of God, however low he may sink, still keeps hold upon his God. "Though he slay me, yet will I trust in him," is the resolution of his soul. Jehovah smites me, but He is my God. Even when He leaves me, I will cry, "My God, my God, why hast thou forsaken me?" (Psalm 22:1), as did our Lord on the Cross of Calvary.

Moreover, the believer in his worst time still continues to pray, and prays, perhaps the more vigorously because of his sorrows. This psalm is full of prayer; it is as much sweetened with supplication as it is salted with sorrow. It weeps like Niobe, but it is on bended knees and from uplifted eyes. Now, while a man can pray, he is never far from light; he is at the window, though, perhaps, as yet the curtains are not drawn aside. The man who can pray has the clue in his hand by which to escape from the labyrinth of affliction. A man must have true and eternal life within him while he can continue still to pray; and while there is such life, there is assured hope.

Exposition of the Text

I will endeavor, in a few observations, to expound the text.

1. Its strong language suggests the remark that *tried saints are very prone to overrate their afflictions*. I believe we all err in that direction, and we are far too apt to say. "I am the man that hath seen affliction." The inspired man of God, who wrote our text, was touched with this common infirmity, for he overstates his case. Read his words: "Thy wrath lieth hard upon me." I have no doubt but that Heman meant wrath in its worst sense. He believed that God was really angry with him, and wrathful with him, even as He is with the ungodly; but

that was not true. As we shall have to show by-and-by, there is a very grave difference between the anger of God with His children and the anger of God with His enemies; and we do not think Heman sufficiently discerned that difference, even as we are afraid that many of God's children even now forget it, and, therefore, fear that the Lord is punishing them according to strict justice, and smiting them as though He were their executioner. Ah, if poor bewildered believers could only see it, they would learn that the very thing which they call wrath is only love, in its own wise manner, seeking their highest good. Besides, the Psalmist saith, "Thy wrath *lieth hard upon me.*" Ah, if Heman had known what it was to have God's wrath lie hard on him, he would have withdrawn that word, for all the wrath that any man ever feels in this life is but as a laying on of God's little finger.

All God's waves have broken over no man, save only the Son of Man. There are still some troubles which we have been spared, some woes to us unknown. Have we suffered all the diseases which flesh is heir to? Are there not modes of pain from which our bodies have escaped? Are there not also some mental pangs which have not wrung our spirit? And what if we seem to have traversed the entire circle of bodily and mental misery, yet in our homes, households, or friendships we have surely some comfort left, and, therefore, from some rough billow we are screened. All God's waves had not gone over thee, O Heman; the woes of Job and Jeremiah were not thine. Among the living, none can literally know what *all* God's waves would be. They know, who are condemned to feel the blasts of his indignation; they know in the land of darkness and of everlasting hurricane; they know what all God's waves and billows are; but we know not. The metaphor is good and admirable, and correct enough poetically, but as a statement of fact, it is strained. We are all apt to aggravate our grief. I say this here as a general fact, which you who are happy can bear to be told; but I would not vex the sick man with it, while he is enduring the weight of his affliction. If he can calmly accept the suggestion of his own accord, it may do him good, but it would be cruel to throw it at him. True as it is, I should not like to whisper it in any sufferer's ear, because it would not console, but it would grieve him.

I have often marvelled at the strange comfort persons offer you when they say, "Ah, there are others who suffer more than you do." Am I a demon then? Am I expected to rejoice at the news of other people's miseries? Far otherwise, I am pained to think there should be sharper smarts than mine; my sympathy increases my own woe. I can conceive of a fiend in torment finding solace in the belief that others are tortured with yet a fiercer flame, but surely such diabolical comfort should not be offered to Christian people. There is, however, a form of comfort akin to it, but of far more legitimate origin; a consolation honorable and divine. There was One upon whom God's wrath pressed very sorely; One who was in truth afflicted with all God's waves, and that One is our brother, a man like ourselves, the dearest lover of our souls; and because He has known and suffered all this, He can enter into sympathy with us this morning, whatever tribulation may beat upon us. His passion is all over now, but not His compassion. He has borne the indignation of God, and turned it all away from us; the waves have lost their fury, and spent their force on Him, our Comforter! As we think of Him, the Crucified, our souls may not only derive consolation from His sympathy and powerful succor, but we may learn to look upon our trials with a calmer eye and judge them more according to the true standard. In the presence of Christ's cross, our own crosses are less colossal. Our thorns in the flesh are as nothing when laid side by side with the nails and spear.

2. Let us remark that *saints do well to trace all their trials to their God.* Heman did so in the text: *"Thy* wrath lieth hard upon me, *thou* hast afflicted me with all *thy* waves." He traces all his adversity to the Lord his God. It is God's wrath; they are God's waves that afflict him, and God makes them afflict him. Child of God, never forget this; all that you are suffering of any sort or kind, comes to you from the divine hand. Truly, you say, "My

affliction arises from wicked men," yet remember that there is a predestination which, without soiling the fingers of the Infinitely Holy, nevertheless rules the motions of evil men as well as of holy angels. It would be a dreary thing for us, if there were no appointments of God's providence which concerned the ungodly; then the great mass of mankind would be entirely left to chance, and the godly might be crushed by them without hope. The Lord, without interfering with the freedom of their wills, rules and overrules, so that the ungodly are as a rod in His hand, with which He wisely scourges His children.

Perhaps you will say that your trials have arisen not from the sins of others, but from your own sin. Even then, I would have you penitently trace them still to God. What if the trouble springs out of sin, yet it is God that has appointed the sorrow to follow the transgression, to act as a remedial agency for your spirit. Look not at the second cause, or, looking at it with deep regret, turn your eye chiefly to your heavenly Father and "hear ye the rod and who hath appointed it" (Micah 6:9). The Lord sends upon us the evil as well as the good of this mortal life; His is the sun that cheers and the frost that chills; His the deep calm and His the fierce tornado. To dwell on second causes is frequently frivolous, a sort of solemn trifling. Men say of each affliction, "It might have been prevented *if* so and so had occurred." Perhaps *if* another physician had been called in, the dear child's life had still been spared; possibly *if* I had moved in such a direction in business I might not have been a loser. Who is to judge of what might have been?

In endless conjectures we are lost, and, cruel to ourselves, we gather material for unnecessary griefs. Matters happened not so; then why conjecture what would have been had things been different? It is folly. You did your best, and it did not answer: why rebel? To fix the eye upon the second cause will irritate the mind. We grow indignant with the more immediate agent of our grief, and so fail to submit ourselves to God. If you strike a dog he will snap at the staff which hurts him, as if *it* were to blame. How doggish we sometimes are, when God is smiting us, we are smarting at His rod. Brother, forgive the man who injured you,—his was the sin, forgive it, as you hope to be forgiven; but yours is the chastisement, and it comes from God, therefore endure it and ask grace to profit by it. When we know "it is the Lord," we readily cry, let Him do what seemeth Him good." As long as I trace my pain to accident, my bereavement to mistake, my loss to another's wrong, my discomfort to an enemy, and so on, I am of the earth, earthly; but when I rise to my God and see His hand at work, I grow calm; I have no word of repining. "Cast thy burden on the Lord" is a precept which it will be easy to practice, when you see that the burden came originally from God.

3. *Afflicted children of God do well to have a keen eye to the wrath that mingles with their troubles.* "Thy *wrath* lieth hard upon me." There is Heman's first point. He does not mention the waves of affliction till he has first spoken of the wrath. We should labor to discover what the Lord means by smiting us; what He purposes by the chastisement, and how far we can answer that purpose. We must use a keen eye clearly *to distinguish* things. There is an anger and an anger, a wrath and a wrath. God is never angry with His children in one sense, but He is in another. As men, all of us have disobeyed the laws of God, and God stands in relationship to all of us as a judge. As a judge, He must execute upon us the penalties of His law, and He must, from the necessity of His nature, be angry with us for having broken that law. That concerns all of the human race. But, the moment a man believes in the Lord Jesus Christ, his offenses are his offenses no longer; they are laid upon Christ Jesus, the substitute, and the anger goes with the sin. The anger of God towards the sins of believers has spent itself upon Christ. Christ has been punished in their stead; the punishment due to their sin has been borne by Jesus Christ.

God forbid that the Judge of all the earth should ever be unjust; it were not just for God to punish a believer for a sin which has been already laid upon Jesus Christ. Hence, the believer is altogether free from all liability to suffer the judicial anger of God, and all risk of receiving a punitive sentence from the Most High. The man is absolved—shall he be judged again? The man has paid the debt—shall he be brought a second time before the judge, as though he were still a debtor? Christ has stood for him in his place and stead, and, therefore, he boldly asks, "Who shall lay anything to the charge of God's elect? It is God that justifieth. Who is he that condemneth? It is Christ that died, yea rather, that is risen again, who is even the right hand of God, who also maketh intercession for us" (Rom. 8:33, 34).

Now, then, the Christian man takes up another position; he is adopted into the family of God: he has become God's child. He is under the law of God's house. There is in every house an economy, a law by which the children and servants are ruled. If the child of God breaks the law of the house, the Father will visit His offense with fatherly stripes—a very different kind of visitation from that of a judge. Wide as the poles asunder are the anger of a judge and the anger of a father. The father loves the child while he is angry, and is mainly angry for that very reason; if it were not his child he would probably take no notice of its fault, but because it is his own boy who has spoken an untruth or committed an act of disobedience, he feels he must chastise him, because he loves him. This needs no further explanation. There is a righteous anger in God's heart towards guilty, impenitent men; He feels none of that towards His people.

Now, child of God, if you are suffering today in any way whatever, whether from the ills of poverty or bodily sickness, or depression of spirits, remember there is not a drop of the judicial anger of God in it all. You are not being punished for your sins as a judge punishes a culprit. Never believe such false doctrine; it is contrary to the truth as it is in Jesus.

But we must use the eye of our judgment in looking at our present affliction to *see and confess* how richly, as children, we deserve the rod. Go back to the time since you were converted, and consider: do you wonder that God chastened you? Speaking for myself, I wonder that I have ever escaped the rod at any time. If I had been compelled to say "All day long have I been plagued, and chastened every morning" (Ps. 73:14), I should not have marvelled, for my shortcomings are many. How ungrateful have we been, how unloving, how unlovable, how false to our holiest vows, and how unfaithful to our most sacred consecrations. Is there a single ordinance over which we have not sinned? Did we ever rise from our knees without having offended while at prayer? Did we ever get through a hymn without some wandering of mind or coldness of heart? Did we ever read a chapter which we might not have wept over, because we did not receive the truth in the love of it into our soul as we ought to have done? O, good Father, if we smart, richly do we deserve that we should yet smart again.

When you have confessed your ill-desert, let me exhort you to use those same eyes zealously to *search out the particular sin* which has caused the present chastisement. "Oh," says one, "I do not think I should ever find it out." You might. Perhaps it lies at the very door. I do not wonder that some Christians suffer; I should wonder if they did not. I have seen them, for instance, neglect family prayer and other household duties; and their sons have grown up to dishonor them. If they cry out, "What an affliction," we would not like to *say,* "Ah, but you might have expected it; you were the cause of it"; but such a saying would be true. When children have left the parental roof and gone into sin, we have not been surprised when the father has been harsh, sour, and crabbed in temper. We did not expect to gather figs of thorns or grapes of thistles. We have seen men whose whole thought was, "Get money, get money," and yet they have professed to be Christians. Such persons have been fretful and unhappy, but we have not been astonished. No, if they walk frowardly with Him, He will show Himself froward to them.

But sometimes the cause of the chastisement lies further off. Every surgeon will tell you that there are diseases which become troublesome in the prime of life, or in old age, which may have been occasioned in youth by some wrong doing, or by accident, and the evil may have lain latent all those years. So may the sins of our youth bring upon us the sorrows of our riper years, and faults and omissions of twenty years ago may scourge us today. I know it is so. If the fault may be of so great an age, it should lead us to more thorough search and to more frequent prayer. Bunyan tells us that Christian met with Apollyon and had such a dark journey through the Valley of the Shadow of Death, because of slips he made when going down the hill into the Valley of Humiliation. It may be so with us. Perhaps when you were young, you were very untender towards persons of a sorrowful spirit; you are such yourself now—your harshness is visited upon you. It may be that, when in better circumstances, you were wont to look down upon the poor and despise the needy; your pride is chastened now. We have seen men who could ride the high horse among their fellow-creatures, and speak very loftily, and when they have been brought very, very low, we have understood the riddle. God will visit His children's transgressions. He will frequently let common sinners go on throughout life unrebuked; but not so His children. If you were going home today and saw a number of boys throwing stones and breaking windows, you might not interfere with them; but if you saw your own lad among them, I am sure you would fetch him out and make him repent of it.

Perhaps the chastisement may be sent by reason of a sin as yet undeveloped—some latent proneness to evil. The grief may be meant to unearth the sin, that you may hunt it down. Have you any idea of what a devil you are by nature? None of us know what we are capable of, if left by grace. We think we have a sweet temper, an amiable disposition! We shall see!! We fall into provoking company, and are so teased and insulted, and so cleverly touched in our raw places, that we become mad with wrath, and our fine amiable temper vanishes in smoke, not without leaving poor testimony behind. Is it not a dreadful thing to be so stirred up? Yes it is, but if our hearts were pure no sort of stirring would pollute them. Stir pure water as long as you like and no mud will rise. The evil is bad when seen, but it was quite as bad when not seen. It may be a great gain to a man to know what sin is in him, for then he will humble himself before his God and begin to combat his propensities. If he had never seen the filth, he would never have swept the house; if he had never felt the pain, the disease would have lurked within; but now that he feels the pain, he will fly to the remedy. Sometimes, therefore, trial may be sent that we may discern the sin within us and confess it.

Now one word of caution! Do not let us expect, when we are in the trouble, to perceive any immediate benefit resulting from it. I have tried myself when under sharp pain to see whether I have grown a bit more resigned, or more earnest in prayer, or more rapt in fellowship with God; and I confess I have never been able to see the slightest trace of improvement at such times, for pain distracts and scatters the thoughts. Remember that word, "Nevertheless, *afterward* it yieldeth the peaceable fruit of righteousness" (Heb. 12:11). The gardner takes his knife and prunes the fruit trees to make them bring forth more fruit; his little child comes trudging at his heels and cries, "Father, I do not see that the fruit comes on the trees after you have cut them." "No, dear child, it is not likely you would; but come round in a few months when the season of fruit has come, and then you shall see the golden apples, which thank the knife." Graces, which are meant to endure, require time for their production.

Exposition of the Benefits of Trouble

Now, I want to give a very short exposition of the benefits of trouble. This is a great subject. Many a volume has been written upon it.

1. *Severe trouble in a true believer has the effect of loosening the roots of his soul earthward and tightening the anchor-hold of his heart heavenward.* How can he love the world which has become so drear to him? Why should

he seek after grapes so bitter to his taste? Should he not now ask for the wings of a dove that he may fly away to his own dear country and be at rest forever? Every mariner on the sea of life knows that, when the soft zephyrs blow, men tempt the open sea with outspread sails; but when the black tempest comes howling from its den, they hurry with all speed to the haven. Afflictions clip our wings with regard to earthly things, so that we cannot fly away from our dear Master's hand, but sit there and sing to Him; but the same afflictions make our wings grow with regard to heavenly things; we are feathered like eagles, we catch the soaring spirit, a thorn is in our nest, and we spread our pinions towards the sun.

2. *Affliction frequently opens truths to us, and opens us to the truth.* I know not which of these two is the more difficult. Experience unlocks truths which else were closed against us; many passages of Scripture will never be made clear by the commentator; they must be expounded by experience. Many a text is written in a secret ink which must be held to the fire of adversity to make it visible. I have heard that you see stars in a well when none are visible above ground, and I am sure you can discern many a starry truth, when you are down in the depths of trouble, which would not be visible to you elsewhere. Besides, I said it opened us to the truth as well as the truth to us. We are superficial in our beliefs: we are often drenched with truth, and yet it runs off from us like water from a marble slab; but affliction, as it were, ploughs us and subsoils us, and opens up our hearts, so that, into our innermost nature the truth penetrates and soaks like rain into ploughed land. Blessed is that man who receives the truth of God into his inmost self; he shall never lose it, but it shall be the life of his spirit.

3. *Affliction, when sanctified by the Holy Spirit, brings much glory to God out of Christians, through their experience of the Lord's faithfulness to them.* I delight to hear an aged Christian giving his own personal testimony of the Lord's goodness. Vividly upon my mind flashes an

event of some twenty-five years ago; it is before me as if it had occurred yesterday, when I saw a venerable man of eighty years, grey and blind with age, and heard him in simple accents, simple as the language of a child, tell how the Lord had led him, and had dealt with him, so that no good thing had failed of all that God had promised. He spoke as though he were a prophet, his years lending force to his words. But suppose he had never known a trial, what testimony could he have borne? Had he been lapped in luxury and never endured suffering, he might have stood there dumb and have been as useful as if he had spoken. We must be tried or we cannot magnify the faithful God, who will not leave His people.

4. *Affliction conforms us to the Lord Jesus.* We pray to be like Christ, but how can we be, if we are not men of sorrows at all, and never become acquainted with grief? Like Christ, and yet never traverse through the vale of tears! Like Christ, and yet have all that heart could wish, and never bear the contradiction of sinners against thyself, and never say, "My soul is exceeding sorrowful, even unto death!" O, sir, thou knowest not what thou dost ask. Hast thou said, "Let me sit on thy right hand in thy Kingdom"? It cannot be granted to you unless you will also drink of His cup and be baptized with His baptism. Share His sorrow, then share His glory.

5. Once more, *our sufferings are of great service to us when God blesses them, for they help us to be useful to others.* It must be a terrible thing for a man never to have suffered physical pain. You say, "I should like to be that man." Ah, unless you had extraordinary grace, you would grow hard and cold; you would get to be a sort of cast-iron man, breaking other people with your touch. No; let my heart be tender, even be soft, if it must be softened by pain, for I would fain know how to bind up my fellow's wound. Let my eye have a tear ready for my brother's sorrows, even if in order to that, I should have to shed ten thousand for my own. As escape from suffering would be an escape from the power to sympathize, and that were

to be deprecated beyond all things. Luther was right, when he said, affliction was the best book in the minister's library. If the man of God who is to minister to others could be always robust, it were perhaps a loss; if he could be always sickly, it might be equally so; but for the pastor to be able to range through all the places where the Lord suffers his sheep to go, is doubtless to the advantage of his flock.

Be thankful then, dear brethren, be thankful for trouble; and above all, be thankful because it will soon be over, and we shall be in the land where these things will be spoken of with great joy. As soldiers show their scars and talk of battles, when they come at last to spend their old age in the country at home; so shall we in the dear land to which we are hastening, speak of the goodness and faithfulness of God, which brought us through all the trials of the way. I would not like to stand in the white-robed host and hear it said, "These are they that come out of great tribulation, all except that one." Would you like to be there to see yourself pointed at as the one saint who never knew a sorrow? We will be content to share the battle, for we shall soon wear the crown and wave the palm.

I know while I am preaching some of you have said, "Ah, these people of God have a hard time of it." So have you. The ungodly do not escape from sorrow by their sin. I never heard of a man escaping from poverty through being a spendthrift. I never heard of a man who escaped from headache or drunkenness or from bodily pain by licentiousness. I have heard the opposite; and if there be griefs to the holy, there are others for you. Only mark this, ungodly ones, mark this. For you these things work no good. You pervert them to mischief; but for the saints, they work eternal benefit. For you your sorrows are punishments; they are not so to the child of God. You are punished for your transgressions, but the child of God is not. And let us tell you, too, that if this day you happen to be in peace and prosperity, plenty and happiness—yet there is not one child of God, in the very depths of trouble that would change places with you under any consideration whatever.

"Let God do as He pleases," we say, "for a while here; we believe our worst state to be better than your best." Do you think we love God for what we get out of Him, and for nothing else? Is that your notion of a Christian's love to God? This is how the ungodly talk, and that is what the devil thought was Job's case. Says he: "Does Job fear God for naught? Hast thou not set a hedge about him, and all that he has?" (Job 1:9, 10). The devil does not understand real love and affection; but the child of God can tell the devil to his face that he loves God if he covers him with sores and sets him on the dunghill, and by God's good help he means to cling to God through troubles tenfold heavier than those he has had to bear, should they come upon him. Is He not a blessed God? Aye, let the beds of our sickness ring with it: He is a blessed God. In the night watches, when we are weary, and our brain is hot and fevered, and our soul is distracted, we yet confess that He is a blessed God. Every ward of the hospital, where believers are found, should echo with that note. A blessed God? "Aye, that He is," say the poor and needy here this morning, and so say all God's poor throughout all the land. A blessed God? "Aye," say His dying people, "as he slays us we will bless His name. He loves us, and we love Him; and, though all His waves go over us, and His wrath lieth sore upon us, we would not change with kings on their thrones, if they are without the love of God."

NOTES

GOD AND THE FACT OF SUFFERING

Sermon One: The Burden of the Mystery
Sermon Two: Lights in the Darkness
Sermon Three: Wearing the Thorns
     as a Crown
Sermon Four: The Cross of Victory

James S. Stewart (1896-) pastored
three churches in Scotland before becoming
professor of theology at the University of
Edinburgh (1936) and then professor of New
Testament (1946). But he is a professor who
can preach, a scholar who can apply biblical
truth to the needs of the common man, and a
theologian who can make doctrine both practical and exciting. He has published several
books of lectures and biblical studies, including *A Man in Christ* and *Heralds of God.*
His two finest books of sermons are *The Gates
of New Life* and *The Strong Name.* This sermon, and the three that follow, are all taken
from *The Strong Name,* published in
Edinburgh in 1940 by T. & T. Clark.

James S. Stewart

5

THE BURDEN OF THE MYSTERY

Have mercy upon me, O Lord, for I am in trouble (Psalm 31:9).
Now is my soul troubled; and what shall I say? (John 12:27).

IN THAT STRANGE medley of a book, *Sartor Resartus,* no passage is more vivid or dramatic than the description of Carlyle's philosopher, gazing out from his high attic across the city at midnight and musing upon the age-long mysteries of life and death, love and suffering, hope and misery. Down beneath him and all around, the dark streets stretch away, where half a million human beings are herded and crammed together—the joyful and the sorrowful, men dying and men being born, some praying and others cursing, women laughing, others weeping, "all these heaped and huddled together, with nothing but a little carpentry and masonry between them," a kind of microcosm of humanity gathered there beneath the covering of the vast, indifferent night. "But I," he concludes, "I sit above it all; I am alone with the Stars."

Is God like that? How many troubled hearts there are today in which that terrible suspicion has begun to rear its head! God seems so remote, so high above this low earth's turmoil and confusion of suffering and darkness and unsolved questions crying out vainly for an answer. Was Celsus, the formidable antagonist of the Church in its early days, perhaps right when he bluntly characterized the Christian doctrine that "God takes an interest in man" as being "an absurd idea"? Was Euripides right, when in his great drama, *The Trojan Women,* he drew that most moving picture of Queen Hecuba, broken-hearted and widowed and childless, with all her world in ruins around her, while the gods on Olympus are too absorbed in other things to hear her bitter cry or even to notice her, where she lies prostrate before them in the dust? Is God like the divinities of Tennyson's *Lotos-Eaters?*

> For they lie beside their nectar, and the bolts are hurl'd
> Far below them in the valleys, and the clouds are lightly curl'd
> Round their golden houses, girdled with the gleaming world:
> Where they smile in secret, looking over wasted lands,
> Blight and famine, plague and earthquake, roaring deeps and fiery sands,
> Clanging fights, and flaming towns, and sinking ships, and praying hands.

"I sit above it all; I am alone with the stars." Is God like that? From Rachel weeping for her children to Jesus suffering on His Cross, from the Trojan queen in her hour of desolation to every troubled heart or home throughout the world today, there rises the insistent question, "Why should this happen? Why should these troubles come? My God, why hast Thou forsaken me?"

There are so many forms of trouble in this world—physical, mental, emotional, spiritual—and the challenge which they severally and collectively present to faith is so radical, that one craves passionately to be able to let in some light upon the darkness. Certainly no one who takes life seriously can escape the necessity of confronting this problem and coming to terms with it in his own soul. It will be worthwhile, therefore, in this and the three succeeding messages, to concentrate our thoughts upon this matter which so deeply concerns us all.

Right at the outset let me say this—that if there is one subject in which the use of any language that is merely facile and conventional must be reckoned as a positive offence, it is this subject of the mystery of suffering. Stock phrases, for instance, like "the nobility of pain," "the uplifting influence of suffering," are very easy to use; but they may simply prove, that the one who uses them has never grasped what the real promise is. Would you go to someone in trouble and say to him piously, "Ah, friend, consider how good this is for your character"? Would you try to heal his wound with tags of commonplace counsel like "Take courage; it might have been worse," or "Don't worry: it may never happen," or "It's a long lane that has no turning"? All that may be true enough; but it has scarce begun to come in sight of the real problem, and it is certainly not within shouting distance of the Christian answer.

The one thing that is quite inexcusable in this whole matter is to be complacent and platitudinous. For when we approach this mystery, we are treading on holy ground. To take but one instance, here are some sentences from a letter which Earl Grey, after his wife's death, wrote to a friend. "I am having a hard struggle. Every day I grasp a little more of all that it means. Just when I have got my spirit abreast of life, I feel and understand more sorrow and sink again. Sometimes it is like a living death; and the perpetual heartache, which has set in, wears me down." Surely in face of troubles like that, it would be far better to be silent than to say things trite and commonplace. Can any attempt indeed to interpret the dark enigma be other than utterly inadequate? Yet even so, one must try to find light enough to walk by. God willing, our quest may not prove quite in vain.

From Where Comes Suffering

Let us, to begin with, be quite clear that in this matter we are not dealing with any merely theoretical conundrum or dilemma. The problem of suffering is urgent and practical—relentlessly so. It is forced upon us from three directions. Briefly let us look at these basic truths.

1. *History* forces it on us. Why, for instance, does God ever permit the unspeakable sufferings and horrors of war? Why, in the name of all that is righteous and true, should this fair earth be desecrated and defiled by such foul and monstrous iniquities of barbarity, persecution, and intolerance as have been witnessed in these days in which we live? You see, the problem of suffering is no longer a thing that can be left to the theorizings of philosophers and theologians, or to the mediations of the aged and infirm: it concerns us all, directly and even violently, in this generation. Very specially it concerns the youth of today. There is no thinking young man or young woman who is not grappling with it. History is forcing it upon us.

2. *Life* forces it upon us. Walk through the wards of a great hospital. Why should there be disease germs? Why should a baby be born blind, or even worse, insane? Why should the innocent suffer? Why are there slums? Why is Nature "red in tooth and claw"? Why are there earthquakes, famines, volcanoes? "You know," cries a young man in one of Hugh Walpole's greatest novels, "you know there can't be a God, Vanessa. In your heart you must know it. You are a wise woman. You read and think. Well, then, ask yourself. How *can* there be a God and life be as it is? If there is one, He ought to be ashamed of Himself, that's all I can say." Life forces the question upon us.

3. *Our own experience* forces it on us. For suffering includes not only physical pain, but all the troubles, disappointments, bereavements, frustrations, to which the human spirit is heir; all the swift, desolating calamities that crash their way through our hopes and dreams; all the slow, subtle disillusionments that steal the heart out of life. It is this aspect of experience, far more than any merely speculative doubt, which is the real threat to faith. Trouble brings many lives face to face with spiritual crisis. How will they react? The answer to the problem of suffering must be no abstract answer in terms of words, but a concrete answer in terms of life.

Now this leads us to the next point—and it is essential that we should get this clear, for it is vitally important, yet often overlooked. Have you noticed that *the first thing Christianity does to the problem of suffering is to heighten and accentuate the difficulty of it?* In fact, it is precisely our Christian faith that creates the problem. There is no real *problem of evil* for the man who has never accepted the Christian revelation. He may recognize, indeed, the fact of suffering; but only to the believer is suffering a mystery. For, you see, only the Christian says "God is love"; therefore, it is only he who has upon his hands and heart the terrible task of squaring the dark, tragic things in life with such a daring declaration of faith. So, in a sense, it is a far worse problem for the believer than for the unbeliever, precisely because of his asseveration of

the love and sovereignty of God. For if there is no God—
just a dead mechanism of a world—then obviously there
is no reason why these dark and evil things should not
happen. They are simply there; there is nothing to explain. But if you assume a God of light and love; then
the question grows acute, and the burden of the mystery
becomes heavy. We do well to face this fact quite frankly,
that the first thing Christianity does with the problem
of suffering is not to solve it, but to heighten and accentuate it.

But having said that, we are entitled to go on at once
and add this—that if the unbeliever escapes the problem
of evil which is so real a mystery to the Christian, he
immediately finds himself encountering another problem,
which, for the Christian, is no mystery at all, namely,
the problem of good. It is certainly hard to explain why,
if God is love, there is no much suffering in the world.
That is the believer's problem. But I submit it would be
even harder to explain why, if there were no God—nothing
but a dead, unspiritual universe—there should be such
facts as self-sacrifice, reverence, nobility, heroism, and
men who will die for their conviction of the right. That
is the unbeliever's problem. And I am sure it is harder
and more insoluble than the other.

Some of you will remember a fragment of conversation from John Galsworthy's *Maid in Waiting:* the
girl Dinny is talking to her mother, Lady Cherwell.
"I suppose there is an eternal Plan," she says, "but
we're like gnats for all the care it has for us as individuals." "Don't encourage such feelings, Dinny,"
says her mother, "they affect one's character." "I
don't see," replies the daughter, "the connection between beliefs and character. I'm not going to behave
any worse because I cease to believe in Providence or
an after life." "Surely, Dinny—" "No; I'm going to
behave *better;* if I'm decent, it's because decency's the
decent thing; and not because I'm going to get anything by it." Whereupon her mother asks, "But why
is decency the decent thing, Dinny, if there's no
God?" That is the ultimate problem.

Why, out of an unspiritual universe, should spiritual facts have arisen? Why is decency the decent thing, if God is a dream? Where did the beauty of a Beethoven sonata come from? Why should Captain Oates have walked out into the blizzard to die, like a hero, for his friends? The unbeliever's scheme of things will allow no answer except that all the loveliness of life, all the fine and noble and heroic things, are—as Bertrand Russell has put it candidly—"the outcome of accidental collocations of atoms," and all the order of the universe the product of blind chance. That, to me, sounds as sensible as to say that you could take a bag full of single letters of the alphabet and throw a few handfuls of them up into the air anyhow and they would fall down in the form of a Shakespeare sonnet or the prologue of St. John. The thing is absurd! Let me put it like this. I, as a believer in God, have to face—as the unbeliever does not—the mystery of the existence of evil. I admit that. But here is the other side of it: the unbeliever has to face—as I, who believe in God, do not—the mystery of the existence of good. And his problem is definitely more insoluble than mine.

Erroneous Reasons For Suffering

Let us, then, take courage and face this problem bravely. I suggest that our next step must be to clear the ground by setting aside once for all certain attempted solutions of the problem which cannot be allowed to stand. I am going to mention three such solutions to you now. You will observe that in each case an element of truth is present—for otherwise they could scarcely have been so vigorously sponsored throughout the centuries. But a few things are so dangerous or misleading as a one-sided truth. Note the following three erroneous ideas.

1. *We must reject the solution that all suffering comes from God.* The element of truth, of course, in that statement is that God has created His world in such a way that sin and suffering are possibilities. But to hold, as some good people do, that God is the direct and immediate cause of everything that happens and, therefore, the cause

of all the evil things that happen—that kind of rigid deter-
minism, that almost mechanical predestination—affronts
our moral sense and makes nonsense of the fact of human
freedom. I am not going to dwell on this now. May I just
remind you of Dr. Samuel Johnson's wise retort when
someone, carried away by the logic of a rigid theory of
predestination, had virtually denied human freedom?
"Sir," said the good Doctor, "we are free, and we know
it, and that is an end of it." The first familiar solution
of our problem must fall to the ground.

2. *We must equally reject the doctrine that all suffering
is due to sin.* The element of truth in that is that all sin
does undoubtedly produce suffering in one form or
another. Indeed, it would be true to say that it is the sin
and folly and bungling and selfishness of men, in history
and down through the ages, which are responsible for a
vast amount of the suffering in the world today. To take
but one modern instance, how much of the international
plight and confusion of recent decades, with all the tragic
consequences of suffering for the individual, were due to
mistaken policies which failed to reflect the true spirit
of Jesus? Can there be any doubt that if, at certain
decisive points in history, there had been a more resolute
attempt to take the ethics of Jesus seriously, to accept
them heartily and to act upon them, much of the chaos
and bitterness which the world has seen could have been
avoided? It is true, in other words, that all sin involves
suffering. But, what I want you to see is that it is not
true to turn that around the other way and suggest (as
some unthinkingly do) that all suffering is due to sin, as
if a man's troubles were necessarily punishments, indications of some flaw in his character.

I am sure it is important to say this quite emphatically;
for I have met people, good people, who, if some great
trouble comes into their life, are made perfectly miserable
by the thought that it must be due to some special sin.
"What have I done that this has happened to me?" But
you cannot equate character and suffering in that way.
Thank God, you need not do it! Long ago, for instance,

when some parts of the Old Testament were written, the idea was that piety and prosperity were in direct proportion to each other and that, therefore, to be visited by trouble and adversity was a sure token that you had been guilty of sin. "Whatsoever he doeth," sang the psalmist of the righteous man, "shall prosper. The ungodly are not so: but are like the chaff which the wind driveth away," (Psalm 1:3, 4).

That, you remember, was precisely the position of Job's friends. There was Job, a mass of suffering. Therefore, said they, he must have sinned terribly; let him confess his sin, and perhaps God would remove his suffering. That was the old orthodox idea. But it was far too simple to be true. It could not fit the facts of life and of experience. And what makes the Book of Job such a vivid drama is that all through it you can see the suffering of man grappling with that false, misleading solution of the mystery, protesting against it, refusing to believe the facile theory of an equivalence between suffering and character, and finally, with agony and travail, wrestling his way through to a deeper and truer answer to his problem. But we can bring in a greater witness than Job. Let us listen to Jesus speaking.

> There were present at that season some that told Him of the Galileans, whose blood Pilate had mingled with their sacrifices. And Jesus answering said unto them, Suppose ye that these Galileans were sinners above all the Galileans, because they suffered such things? I tell you, Nay . . . Or those eighteen, upon whom the tower in Siloam fell, and slew them, think ye that they were sinners above all men that dwell in Jerusalem? I tell you, Nay . . . (Luke 13:1-5).

That is plain enough. Here you have it, on the authority of Jesus, that it is a false simplification to say that all suffering is due to sin. And there was another day, you remember, when Jesus and His disciples met a man who had been blind from birth: and the disciples asked Jesus (notice the old rigid idea of an equivalence between sin and suffering coming out again almost instinctively), "Master, who did sin, this man, or his parents, that he was born blind?" And Christ answered, "Neither hath this man sinned, nor his parents," (John 9:23). Therefore, my friend, if you have been vexing your soul with the idea that some suffering of yours is necessarily a punishment visited on you by God because of sin, it is Christ who has given me authority to bid you put that dreadful thought away. This is the second false solution of the mystery of suffering which we must resolutely set aside.

3. Finally, *we must reject the theory that all suffering is an illusion.* The element of truth here is that a good many of our pains and troubles are in the mind mainly. They are mentally conditioned. They can be traced back to familiar and ascertainable psychological causes. They are not objectively real. We conjure them up ourselves. It is our mental attitude that creates them. No doubt many troubles are like that. But what exaggeration to say that all suffering is of this kind! Think of the dark tragedies in the earth at this moment—ruined homes, oppressions of the weak by the strong, cries of orphaned children, squalid slums, defeats in business, disappointments in love, broken hearts—is all that mere appearance? Mark you, if they are, then all the heroisms men and women have produced in facing sufferings such as these have been unsubstantial and quixotic. Will you say that? Were the martyrs at the stake playing a game? Was Jesus in His Passion week just acting? Is the good fight of faith mere make-believe? Will you go to a man who has lost his limb in an accident, and say to him, "Buck up, old fellow, it isn't real"? Or to a desolate mother who has lost a child, and say, "Your suffering is in the mind only—you'll get over it"?

There are systems of thought today, modern theosophies, whose gospel is that all suffering is an illusion. I say these systems are an affront to the intelligence and an offence to the heart. I have seen a child crying over a broken toy as if its heart would break. Is that trouble an illusion? Only one with no understanding of childhood would dream of saying that. It is real—and it matters. And we poor humans, with our broken pathetic toys and desolating sorrows—are we imagining things? Do you think God would allow His children to go on indefinitely being mocked with an age-long illusion, being deceived and made tragically unhappy by what was nothing more than a figment of their own foolish, fevered imagination? What a poor, ungodlike jest! To say that all suffering is illusion would be like asking a man who had just lost his wife to come to the theatre, or suggesting to someone who is desperate with a guilty conscience that all he needs is a game of golf. No, you do not dismiss the challenge of the mystery of trouble with a wave of the hand, nor with the easy verdict of a superficial optimism which says, "The thing is unreal." It is as real as the stones that killed Stephen, as real as the nails they drove into the flesh of Christ. This third familiar explanation we must unhesitatingly reject.

What, then, are we to say? The search for a solution must be continued. This present study has been in the nature of clearing of the ground for something more positive to follow. It may be, of course, that we shall find there is no complete and final answer to the mystery of suffering. It may be we shall have to confess that to understand the mystery fully, we should require to look out upon life with the eyes of God Himself. In other words, we may be led to conclude that there will always, to the very end of the day, be need for an act of sheer naked faith. If that is so, we need not be ashamed. Faith requires no apology. And in any case, if it is faith in God which creates the problem (as we have already seen reason to maintain), it is surely understandable that it is only faith in God which is going to answer it.

In the next chapter I invite you to consider some beams of light upon the darkness of the mystery. "If I from my spy-hole," wrote Robert Louis Stevenson, "looking upon a fraction of the universe, yet perceive some broken evidences of a plan, shall I be so mad as to complain that all cannot be deciphered?" I think the attempt to solve the enigma is rather like learning a foreign language. You read a page and you understand perhaps only a word or two here and there; but, you do not on that account say—"This book is nonsense! It has no meaning." You say, "Because I recognize a word here and there, I am sure all the rest makes sense. And one day I shall understand." Yes, even now there are traces of a plan, beams of light flung out across the darkness. It is these that we must now try to follow. And it may be we shall come to see our darkness, if not dispelled, at least redeemed and robbed of all its fears by one light, far steadier and brighter than all the rest: the light of the love and victory of God on the face of Jesus Christ.

GOD AND THE FACT OF SUFFERING

Sermon One: The Burden of the Mystery
Sermon Two: Lights in the Darkness
Sermon Three: Wearing the Thorns
              as a Crown
Sermon Four: The Cross of Victory

James S. Stewart (1896-   ) pastored
three churches in Scotland before becoming
professor of theology at the University of
Edinburgh (1936) and then professor of New
Testament (1946). But he is a professor who
can preach, a scholar who can apply biblical
truth to the needs of the common man, and a
theologian who can make doctrine both practical and exciting. He has published several
books of lectures and biblical studies, including *A Man in Christ* and *Heralds of God*.
His two finest books of sermons are *The Gates
of New Life* and *The Strong Name*. This sermon, and the three that follow, are all taken
from *The Strong Name*, published in
Edinburgh in 1940 by T. & T. Clark.

James S. Stewart

6

LIGHTS IN THE DARKNESS

Who is among you that feareth the Lord, that walketh in darkness and hath no light? let him trust in the name of the Lord, and stay upon his God. (Isaiah 50:10).
Unto the upright there ariseth light in the darkness (Psalm 112:4).

THERE IS A very moving scrap of conversation near the beginning of *Pilgrim's Progress* by John Bunyan. Poor burdened Christian had met Evangelist and begged for help and guidance. Whereupon, Evangelist pointed to the far distance, and asked, "Do you see yonder wicket-gate?" Christian looked, shook his head, and answered, "No." Then Evangelist tried again. "Do you see yonder shining light?" he asked. And Christian peered away to the far horizon and noticed something—one spot that seemed not quite so dark as all the rest; and he answered, "I think I do." "Keep that light in your eye," said Evangelist, "and go up directly thereto, so shalt thou see the gate."

I fancy that if someone inquired of you or me, "Do you see the answer to the riddle of life and the mystery of sorrow?" we should have to answer, as bluntly as Christian did, "No, I do not see it." But if the inquirer went on to ask, "Do you see any points of light, any places where the darkness of the mystery is not quite so dark as elsewhere?" some of us, with Christian, would reply, "I think I do." It is some of these beams of light that I invite you to consider now. It may be that if we keep them before us and trust their guiding, we, too, may "see the gate." For the darkness in which we walk is not impenetrable gloom; and the night—thank God—has stars.

Beams of Light

1. The first beam of light is what I would call *the beneficence of inexorable law.*

It is perfectly clear that a good deal of the tragic element in life is due to the working of certain uniform principles which govern the universe. There is the law of gravitation, for instance. That law means that a child who wanders too near the edge of a precipice may be killed; that an airplane whose engine fails may crash. But the point to notice is this—that the same laws which are responsible for so much human suffering are also the indispensable sources of most of the things that make life worth living.

Does it not begin to lighten at least the burden of the mystery when we grasp that? The fact of the matter is that even though the physical laws of the universe may often work out tragically for human beings, yet, for all that, we would not choose, even if we could, to live in a world without these laws: for then our predicament would be infinitely worse than it is now.

Gravitation, as I have said, may mean the death of a child or the crash of an airplane. It may mean scores of accidents and disasters every day. But remember this: without gravitation, you could not walk along the street, you could not travel in a train, you could not launch a ship, you could not span a river with a bridge. Life would simply become unlivable.

Or, think of fire. It is an inexorable property of fire that it gives out heat. And that very property may mean some day that a hundred people, trapped in a blazing building, are burnt to death. What then? Do you wish that fire would not behave like that? Then it would cease to be fire, and all its tremendous contribution to human welfare and well-being would be lost. You cannot have it both ways.

Take even grim facts like earthquakes and volcanoes. It is hard to discover any trace of beneficence there. But, the fact is that the very forces which occasionally produce these devastating outbursts are the same forces which, working continually beneath the earth's surface, make and keep this planet habitable for the sons of men.

You cannot have all the assets of life and refuse its liabilities. The uniformity of Nature, the inexorableness of law, may cause us tragic sufferings: but if Nature were not uniform, if law were not inexorable, we should not be here at all, either for happiness or for woe, for life would be impossible.

Here is how the late Canon Streeter illustrated the point. The pressure of law, he suggested, is "like the immovability of the goal-line, without which there could be no game, though it would at times be vastly convenient to an individual player, if by a miracle the line would approach or retire a yard or two." Picture that football player racing toward the goal-line with the ball. The opposing backs come out to tackle him. How opportune it would be for the man with the ball if the goal-line were movable—if it would suddenly bend back in the nick of time and let him cross it! And yet, you can see that it is on the rigidity of the goal-line that the whole game depends; there could be no game without it. So in the serious business of life. Sometimes it would facilitate things vastly for the individual player, for you and me, if the laws of Nature would bend back and let us dodge them. We all wish feverishly that they would do that sometimes. And yet, can you not see that it is upon the absolute fixity of that line, the rigidity of that law, that the whole game depends? What kind of universe would it be in which Nature were erratic and capricious? What kind of a world in which the law of gravitation operated one moment and not the next? It would be a madhouse of a world. Of such a world Othello's cry would be strictly true, "Chaos is come again." It would be quite impossible to get ahead with the business of life. The rigid laws of God's universe may hit us sorely sometimes; but if that is the price we have to pay for being delivered from the terrifying alternative, every soul of us would say, "It is worth the price!" Robert Browning knew what he was talking about when he cried, "All's love yet all's law!" There, then, shines our first beam of light upon the mystery—the beneficence of inexorable law.

2. The second beam of light is what the Apostle Paul described as *our membership one of another.*

There is no question that much of the innocent suffering in this world is due to the fact that we are all so inextricably mixed up together. If one man plays the fool, a dozen, or a score, or a thousand may be ruined. If one country breaks faith, the whole world may be plunged in cataclysm. That is manifestly true. But over against it you have to set this countervailing consideration, that the very fact—our mutual interdependence—which is responsible for so much of the sheer tragedy of life, is also responsible for life's greatest glory.

And again I ask you, does it not begin to lighten the burden of the mystery, when you realize that—even if this corporate relationship of mankind is the cause of half our troubles—there is not one of us who would choose, even if he could, to stand outside that relationship; for then our human prospect would be infinitely darker than it is?

Perhaps someone says, "I do not agree. I should be much better off, standing for myself alone! Why should life compel me, to be intermeshed, bound up in the same bundle with thousands of other people, and to be involved in all their blunderings, follies and futilities? Why should I not break away, and stand isolated, free, master of my fate and captain of my soul?"

But wait a moment. There is another side to it. Suppose you got your way. Suppose that this troublous and highly dangerous fact of being members one of another were eliminated. Suppose you were an isolated unit. Then, certainly, you would escape hundreds of the things you suffer now. But think what you would lose! Think what you owe to this perilous fact of belonging to the human fellowship. The bread you eat, the clothes you wear, the coals you burn, the scientific discoveries you use, the books you read, the medical help you call in when you are ill—they have all come to you through other men's labors. All the assets of the infinitely complex human relationship are yours. So again I say—you must not try to have it both ways. This fact of mankind as a brotherhood is double-edged: you cannot accept the assets and disown the liabilities; you cannot share the blessings and shirk the risks. And if it came to be a choice between having a place in the corporate fellowship, with all the sufferings which that entails, and contracting out and standing on your own in naked isolation, there is no sane man who would hesitate one moment. "It is worth the price," he would say, bowing his back to humanity's burden, "it is gloriously worth the price!" Clear through the midnight darkness of the mystery gleams this steady light: our membership one of another.

3. The third beam of light which shines out for me is *the wisdom of the divine impartiality.*

Look at it like this. Most of us would say that the real crux of the whole problem of evil, the cruel sting of the thing, is the absolutely indiscriminate way in which trouble falls on saint and sinner alike. It aims its blows with appalling indifference at those who deserve them and at those who do not deserve them in the least. There was an earthquake in India. It knocked down a mission-house and left standing, just a few doors down the street, an opium-den. In that mission-house, for years, souls of men and women had been getting saved; in the opium-den, for years, souls had been getting damned. Yet the earthquake destroyed the mission, and spared the den. And we want to ask, Why? Why should it not have been the other way round? Would it not be a better universe if we could be sure that virtue would reap its appropriate reward, and vice its appropriate pain? It is this dreadful indifference that is the problem, this appalling impartiality that baffles us! What are we to say of a world which enthrones a Herod, and crucifies a Christ?

Let us go to our New Testament on this point. What has the Gospel to say about it? At first sight, the Gospel has very little comfort to give. It does not say that, if a man follows Christ, his business will not go bankrupt. It does not suggest that, if two parents believe sincerely in God, death will never rob them of a child. It does not hold out a promise that, if you are a religious man, there will always be supernatural intervention to lift you out of every tight corner—like the *deux ex machina,* the "God from the machine," of the old Greek plays. Jesus once told a story about two houses, the one built by a wise man, the other by a fool; and Jesus said that on both these houses—which meant, on both these lives, the saint's no less than the sinner's—"the rain descended, and the floods came, and the winds blew and beat" (Matthew 7:35). And our puzzled hearts cry, Why? Would not the world be far more just and divine if evil got its deserts and goodness went immune?

But think again. Would it? I am sure that on second thought you will see that a world like that would be definitely less divine, far more trying, than the actual world in which we live today. For it would mean that the laws of the universe would have to be suspended or interrupted every time a good man was in danger or in difficulty; and that (as we have seen already) would simply lead to chaos. Moreover, (and this is even more crucial) an inevitable corollary of a universe in which penalties and rewards were invariably dealt out in direct ratio to vice and virtue would be the despiritualizing of religion and the ruin of character. For if a Christian escaped the troubles that visit other folk, if religion "got you off," you can see what would almost be bound to happen: religion would become a kind of gigantic insurance policy—a commercial transaction, a *quid pro quo*—and you would have people paying the premium for the sake of the insurance. And that would be the ruin of religion and character forever. No, far better that troubles should come, and darkness descend, and the heavens crash and fall, than that righteousness should be sought for any reason except for righteousness' sake alone. That is another star, shining aloft to illuminate our darkness—the wisdom of the divine impartiality.

4. There is a fourth beam of light we can discern: *the awakening of the conscience of humanity.*

It is of vital importance to get this clear. Must we not believe that one main function of the face of the suffering which we encounter all around us is to be a perpetual challenge to us to be up and doing, to be cooperating with a burden-bearing God, and to be giving ourselves in con-

secrated service for the healing of this broken earth? If
the sight of suffering is indeed having that effect upon
us, then the sorrows of those who suffer will not have been
in vain: they will have contributed something positive.
For they will have helped to stab the human conscience
wide awake and to send us out crusading for a better and
happier tomorrow and for a world nearer to the mind and
will of God.

I think, for instance, of facts like poverty, unemployment, and war, and of the cruel agonies which these en-
tail. Now if poverty, unemployment, and war were the
will of God, then, of course, we should simply have to accept them. There would be no call for us to do anything
about them, or to stir a finger to remove the sufferings
they bring. But if these things are not the will of God at
all, but simply the product of human bungling and
selfishness and sin; and if, accordingly, God's mind and
program for the race is that they should one day be
banished from the earth, then clearly we are not meant
to lie down under them and accept them with resignation. Every man, woman and child who is enduring
anguish today from the results of poverty, unemployment,
or war is contributing something to the total challenge
which comes to us like an urgent divine summons and
incentive to get on with the work of world-rebuilding.

For consider: What do we expect to happen? Do we suggest that because poverty, unemployment, and war are
clearly contrary to the will of God, therefore God
Himself—without waiting for anything else—should suddenly intervene and remove them? But, surely what is
involved in the very fact on which we have already
dwelt—the fact that God deliberately chose to make His
children a fellowship and not separate units—is that He
means us to be the agents of His purpose, and the chan-
nels of His providence to one another. It would be wrong
for a father to do all his boy's homework for him while
the boy idled and played. And it would be hurtful and
disastrous if our Father in heaven were to solve all our
troubles for us and land us in the New Jerusalem, while
we sat looking on. No, God's work waits upon the

awakening of man's conscience and the dedicating of his heart and hands in willing service.

Mark you, this assertion does not (as some timidly protest) dim the glory of God by hinting at a failure in omnipotence, a slur upon the divine sovereignty. For the fact is that it is God Himself who, in His sovereign wisdom, has chosen to have it so.

Hence, we may say that those who suffer need never feel that their pain and grief and trouble are quite negative and unmeaning. They are doing the work of God by getting the conscience of mankind awake. In that sense, the sufferers of today are bearing the burden for the unborn generations of tomorrow; the cross they carry now is contributing to the final liberation of the race; their vicarious Via Dolorosa is the highroad to the city of God. "Let They work appear unto Thy servants, and Thy glory unto their children" (Psalm 90:16). That is a real light on the darkness of the mystery.

We have thought in this connection of poverty, unemployment, and war; but there is one fact we dare not miss, the grim fact of sickness and disease. "Why," we ask, "does God allow that? Why does He permit the things which are everyday occurrences in our hospitals? Why does He not come in and, by one word of His mouth, heal all those dreadful ills and disabilities to which the flesh is heir? Clearly, they cannot be His will, for on almost every page of the Gospels you see Jesus fighting the scourge of disease and refusing to be resigned to it. And if it is not His will, why does He not remove it now?"

It may not be all the answer, but it is part of the answer at least—that here, as in other cases of poverty, unemployment, and war, God means *us* to be the messengers of His providence to others. Here as there, God's will waits upon the arousing of the conscience of His children. It is safe to say that, if the conscience of the world were sufficiently awakened to spend on the constructive, glorious work of eliminating disease and promoting health, one-twentieth of what the world is actually spending now on the negative and horrible work of creating implements of death and devastation, nearly all the scourges of sickness and disease would be gone from the earth in a decade.

Certainly, we have no right to blame God for not removing sickness and disease, as long as man goes on destructively squandering the very resources for their removing, which God has put into his hands. Let us pray, rather, that the conscience of humanity may be awakened and aroused. Let us thank God for every token of that awakening we encounter. With the vast spectacle of the world's suffering confronting us, let us resolve before God that we at least shall be awake to our responsibility, realizing our function as mediators of His will and providence to our fellow-men. And let us meanwhile recognize that all the tragedies of this earth—by challenging the conscience of humanity—are making a positive contribution to the redeeming of the world; and that those who suffer and who sorrow are fellow-laborers with God in the bearing of that age-long cross by which at the end of the day all sufferings shall be mended and all sorrows lose themselves in perfect joy. This is our fourth beam of light—the awakening of the conscience of humanity.

There for the present we must leave it. Nothing has been said as yet about a fifth light, perhaps the greatest of them all, namely, the power of sorrow and trouble to chisel the spirit and beautify the character and deepen the whole tone of life. Something of that we shall see in our next study.

Yet, must we not admit quite frankly that if these gleams of light we have been noticing were all the answer that could be given; if the very best one could do for a soul in trouble were to dwell upon the beneficence of inexorable law, our membership one of another, the wisdom of the divine impartiality, and the awakening of the conscience of humanity—if that were the sum-total of the comfort to be offered, one would hardly have the heart to dwell upon it at all? For what men and women want most in the hour of trouble is not an answer to a problem, but a power to carry them through. And, indeed, even if the best and most completely satisfying solution of the mystery of suffering were available, that would not alter the fact that the actual suffering itself—the grim reality in experience—would still be there to be endured.

So, we begin to see that there is a deeper question than Why?—namely, How? The ultimate demand is not "Why has this happened to me?" but "How, seeing it *has* happened, am I to face it?" And when you see that, suddenly the New Testament comes right in. The New Testament is not much concerned about Why?—because it knows that that is not the basic question. But it is desperately and magnificently concerned about How? It does not offer you a theory and an explanation: *it offers you a power and a victory.*

Thus far in our study we have been lingering in the forecourt of the Temple, for even the forecourt is not without its messages for mind and conscience. But now we must press right in, until we reach the Holy Place; and there we shall see, coming forth to meet us, God's answer—when we lift our eyes and gaze upon a cross.

NOTES

GOD AND THE FACT
OF SUFFERING

Sermon One: The Burden of the Mystery
Sermon Two: Lights in the Darkness
**Sermon Three: Wearing the Thorns
as a Crown**
Sermon Four: The Cross of Victory

James S. Stewart (1896-   ) pastored
three churches in Scotland before becoming
professor of theology at the University of
Edinburgh (1936) and then professor of New
Testament (1946). But he is a professor who
can preach, a scholar who can apply biblical
truth to the needs of the common man, and a
theologian who can make doctrine both practical and exciting. He has published several
books of lectures and biblical studies, including *A Man in Christ* and *Heralds of God*.
His two finest books of sermons are *The Gates
of New Life* and *The Strong Name*. This sermon, and the three that follow, are all taken
from *The Strong Name*, published in
Edinburgh in 1940 by T. & T. Clark.

James S. Stewart

7

WEARING THE THORNS AS A CROWN

Though He were a Son, yet learned He obedience by the things
which He suffered (Hebrews 5:8).

LET ME SET down two incidents as giving the keynote for
our thoughts in this chapter.

In one of George Macdonald's books, there is a woman
who has met a sudden sorrow. "I wish I'd never been
made!" she exclaims petulantly and bitterly; to which her
friend quietly replies, "My dear, you're not made yet.
You're only being made—and this is the Maker's process."
The other incident is from a play of Ibsen's. "Who taught
thee to sing?" one of the characters asks another. And
the answer comes—"God sent me sorrow."

Here, then, we come in sight of this lovely and
momentous fact—that in the making of the soul and in
the producing of life's deepest and profoundest harmonies,
suffering has a positive and creative function to fulfil.
This is the truth which Elizabeth Browning, in a sonnet
entitled "Perplexed Music," has beautifully expressed:

> We murmur,—'Where is any certain tune
> Or measured music, in such notes as these?'—
> But angels, leaning from the golden seat,
> Are not so minded; their fine ear hath won
> The issue of complete cadences."

Let us recall the path our thoughts have travelled up
to this point. We passed in review three familiar solutions of the mystery which respectively trace all suffering
back to God, to sin, to an illusion in the human mind;
and each of these was rejected, being inadequate to meet
the facts. Then, we went on to ask whether, even if the
darkness lingered, we could not at least discern some
beams of light to penetrate the shadows; and four such
beams we found—the beneficence of inexorable law, the

significance of our membership one of another, the wisdom of the divine impartiality, and the awakening of the human conscience. We agreed that while much of the tragedy of life is clearly due to the inexorable working of the laws which govern the universe, to the fact that we are all so inextricably mixed up together, and to the indiscriminate and impartial way in which trouble falls on saint and sinner alike—we agreed that we would not choose, even if we could, to live in a world whose laws were not thus rigid and dependable; nor in a world where we could stand as isolated units, instead of being members one of another; nor in a world where God favored the righteous, and exempted good people from trouble, and so made religion an insurance policy for those who would pay the premium. We say that, in a world like that, our predicament would be far worse than in this actual, present world about whose government we so readily and, perhaps, so unthinkingly, complain. Finally, we decided that it was a main purpose of the sight of suffering to stab the conscience of humanity awake and to constrain us to realize our function as agents of God's providence to our fellowmen. These four beams of light in the darkness we discovered.

But now, as we continue on our road towards the final Christian answer, there is a *fifth light* which flashes out before us: and I cannot but believe that, in speaking of this, one must be speaking to all. It is *the gift* which *suffering brings to character, the contribution trouble makes to the moulding and shaping and beautifying of the soul.* Even of Jesus it stands written that "He learned obedience by the things He suffered."

You will be aware that in pondering this deep matter, we are standing on holy ground and dealing with experiences most intimate and sacred. Here our thoughts begin to converge upon the very heart of the mystery. Let me endeavor, for the sake of clarity, to take the truth which emerges at this point of our inquiry and cast it into the form of three propositions.

The Gift Which Suffering Brings

1. The first is this: *It takes a world with trouble in it to make possible some of the finest qualities of life.* You do not need to be an art connoisseur to realize that it is an essential of a good picture that in it there should be shadow as well as light. You do not need to be a Bach or a Beethoven to understand how a discord can add excitement and beauty to a harmony. Now life is like that. If there were no risk and danger in life, where would fortitude and chivalry be? If there were no suffering, would there be compassion? If there were no discipline and hardship, would we ever learn patience and endurance? Construct a universe with no trouble in it, and immediately you banish some of the finest qualities in the world.

It is possible to go even further and say, If there were no fierce temptations, where would righteousness be? If there were no demons of darkness to be fought, where would be moral fibre or the thrill of victory? "My temptations," said Martin Luther, "have been my masters in divinity." Do you remember William James' comment on the famous picture by Guido Reni in the Louvre which shows Michael with his foot on Satan's throat? "The world," mused James, "is all the richer for having a devil in it, *so long as we keep our foot upon his neck*"—a daring thought indeed, but you can see the truth behind it. It is the truth which the Apostle James taught when he cried, "Count it all joy when ye fall into divers temptations" (James 1:2). Relax life's discipline, remove its hardness, and who among us would be safe? Eliminate from our environment every element of difficulty and toughness and recalcitrance, and spiritual degeneration will not be long postponed. We know our own hearts well enough to realize the truth of this. And so, in the words of a fine poem by Aubrey de Vere:

> Count each affliction, whether light or grave,
> God's messenger sent down to thee; do thou
> With courtesy receive him; rise and bow;
> And, ere his shadow cross thy threshold, crave
> Permission first his heavenly feet to lave;
> Then lay before him all thou hast.

If life is a warfare in which there is no discharge, an unceasing vigilance, a road beset with dangers, often rough and arduous and thorny, often darkened and obscure, always winding uphill steeply right on to the journey's end—let us not grumble and complain and indulge in petulant self-pity: let us, rather, thank God for it. For that is how souls are made. It takes a world with trouble in it to make possible some of the finest qualities in life.

2. Our second proposition is this: *It takes a world with trouble in it to satisfy man's demand for a dangerous universe.* I am sure the human heart's instinct for adventure is a real factor in the situation. We do not merely accept the fact of a world which has the potential of trouble in it: we positively ask for it. From Abraham going out with the morning in his eyes, to Madame Curie wresting from Nature the secret of radium; from a small company of men in an upper room proposing to turn the world upside down, to the cancer-research student in a biological laboratory—the passion for adventure haunts the human spirit. Man knows that a hazardous universe is better far than any lotus-land of flabby and monotonous ease.

You will remember Aldous Huxley's picture, in *Brave New World,* of such a land, where all the harsh and cutting actualities of life have been magically cancelled out and the intrusion of pain and trouble is unknown. "It is Christianity without tears," proudly declares the Controller, explaining his secret. "But," cries another voice, "the tears are necessary. You get rid of them. You just abolish the slings and arrows. It's too easy. I don't want comfort. I want God. I want poetry. I want real danger. I want freedom." "But," says the Controller, "you'll be very unhappy." "I claim," retorts the other, "the right to be unhappy!" That is a real instinct of human spirit. Did not Lessing, the great philosopher, declare that if God came to him, offering in His right hand the whole of truth, and in His left the search for truth and all the toil and travail and mistakes of the search, he would choose the left and say, "Lord, give me that!"—not the finished article, but the zest and tang and danger of the quest? Did Sir J.M. Barrie not say on one occasion, speaking of his youth, "The greatest glory that ever came to me was to be swallowed up in London, not knowing a soul, with no means of subsistence, and the fun of working until the stars went out"? And did not a greater than Barrie cry:

> I would hate that death bandaged my eyes, and forbore
> And bade me creep past.
> No! let me taste the whole of it?

That is a native element of the human spirit. "The kingdom of heaven," exclaimed James Denney, "is not for the well-meaning: it is for the desperate!" And when we chide and censure God for creating a world which contains so many possibilities of grief and suffering, let us remember that there is that within us which craves risk and that it takes an environment with trouble in it to satisfy man's demand for a dangerous universe.

3. The third proposition is this: *It takes a world with trouble in it to train men for their high calling as sons of God, and to carve upon the soul the linaments of the face of Christ.* Have you ever watched a child facing one of those minor, desolating tragedies: the breaking of a favorite doll or the loss of some precious childish treasure? What utter, overwhelming grief! The whole world, to the child, looks black. But, you, who take that little one to your arms to comfort his sad tears away, know that his pitiful little calamity is not all loss and darkness: for that is just life beginning those incomparably important lessons which can be learned no easier way. And I think that often our heavenly Father, looking down at the griefs and troubles and heartbrakes of us, His little children, knows—even while He takes us to His everlasting arms to comfort us—that our day of darkness is not, as we may think, sheer rack and ruin, but irreplaceably profitable for the growth and making of the soul.

A professor of music in Vienna said a startling thing about a pupil of his own. "She is a magnificent singer," he said, "and yet there's just something lacking in her singing. Life has been too kind to her. But if one day it happened that some one broke her heart, she would be the finest singer in Europe!" A crude, even callous, way of putting it: yet was there no truth there? Has it not frequently been pointed out that the word "strain" has a double meaning? It means stress, suffering, trouble; but it means also music; it means song. Is there a connection?

Life says there is. "I have known," said Ralph Erskine, lying racked with pain, "more of God since I came to this bed than through all my life." "The darkness," exclaimed Kagawa of Japan, describing what it felt like when he thought he was going blind, "the darkness is a holy of holies of which no one can rob me. In the darkness I meet God face to face." And here is this amazing statement in *Hebrews*, surely one of the most daring summaries of the life of Jesus ever penned: "Though He were a Son, yet learned He obedience by the things which He suffered."

Here, I suspect, lies the clue to this striking and astonishing fact—that the problem of evil is raised far more often by the spectators of life than by the actual combatants. You will nearly always find that the loudest voices railing against providence and the universe—the voices which keep crying out noisily, "How can there be a God and life be so tragic and unjust?"—belong to the spectators of life's sufferings, and not to the sufferers themselves. You will hardly ever find that the great sufferers are the great skeptics. Quite the reverse. It is the spectators, the people who are outside, looking at the tragedy, from whose ranks the skeptics come; it is not those who are actually in the arena and who know suffering from the inside. Indeed, the fact is that it *is* the world's greatest sufferers who have produced the most shining examples of unconquerable faith. It is precisely from the company of the sons and daughters of affliction that the most convinced believers of all the ages have sprung.

Who are the men whose names stand on the dramatic roll-call of the faithful in the Epistle to the *Hebrews*. Are they men whose days were happy and unclouded and serene; souls for whom the sun was always shining and the skies unvisited by storm or midnight? If any one imagines that such is the background of faith, let him listen to this—"They were stoned, they were sawn asunder, were tempted, were slain with the sword...being destitute, afflicted, tormented; they wandered in deserts, and in mountains, and in dens and caves of the earth" (Heb. 11:37, 38). That, declares the New Testament, has been in every age faith's grim heredity! And it is not from sheltered ways and quiet, sequestered paths; it is from a thousand crosses that the cry ascends—"Hallelujah! For the Lord God omnipotent reigneth." "The bird on the branch," wrote Kierkegaard, "the lily in the meadow, the stag in the forest, the fish in the sea, and countless joyful people sing: God is love! But under all these sopranos, as it were a sustained bass part, sounds the *de profundis* of the sacrificed: God is love."

What can be the reason? Must it not be this, that suffering initiates the soul into secrets which the mere onlooker can never know? Here, at any rate, it is not true to say that the spectators see most of the game. They see less than half the game. They see the clouds and darkness and mystery and tragedy, and so they bombard heaven with their petulant accusations and shout at God their resentful "Why? Why? Why?" But the sufferers themselves are not like that: they are not caring to raise the question, for they have made discoveries—through their sufferings—which are better than any answer.

> I walked a mile with Pleasure.
>   She chattered all the way,
> But left me none the wiser
>   For all she had to say.
>
> I walked a mile with Sorrow,
>   And ne'er a word said she;
> But, oh, the things I learned from her,
>   When Sorrow walked with me!

I want you to verify this from your own experience. If some recording angel of God were to visit all our homes today, and we were asked individually to name the experiences which have blessed and taught us most, the influences which have brought the greatest enrichment to our spirits, would it be the happy, carefree hours that the majority of us would mention first? Surely that angel's book, when he had finished with his task, would tell a very different tale. It would tell, of course, of enrichment brought by God's great gifts of love, home, nature, and the beauty of the world; but page after page there would be to tell how trouble, difficulty, bereavement, bitter disappointment, hopes frustrated, and dreams that flickered out and died—all the things which hurt and leave a mark—had brought blessing, by imparting new depth, new insight, to the soul. And these words that stand written in our text of God's first-born child Jesus, God Himself may be using as He looks upon others of His children here today: "Son though He was, yet learned He by what He suffered."

Is not this the great transfiguring discovery, that pain can be creative? You do not just have to bear it negatively; you can use it positively. You can force it not to subtract, but to add on, something to your total experience. You can take what has all the appearance of being an ugly implement of destruction, and transform it into the loveliest weapon in all your armory for the good of faith. This is what that modern saint von Hugel meant when he spoke about "grasping life's nettle." You can realize, like Paul, that the "thorn in the flesh," the thing which you feel inclined to call (as he did, to begin with) "the messenger of Satan to buffet me," is really not that, but Christ's own angel in disguise. By the grace of God, you can compel the darkest, bitterest experiences to yield up their hidden treasures of sweetness and light. And be very sure of this—no sorrow will have been wasted, if you come through it with a little more of the light of the Lord visible in your face and shining in your soul.

Suppose you had the power to turn back the pages of the volume of the years and make a new beginning; suppose that the recording angel came to you today and said, "Here is your life—I am going to let you go back ten years, twenty years, forty years, and start all over again," what would you say? Would you ask that the sorrows and hardships you have had should this time be eliminated? No, surely not: for if these things were put away, how much poorer you would be! Leave it to Omar Khayyam and all his tribe of hedonistic sentimentalists to rail at "this sorry scheme of things" and to want a world with only pleasure in it and all the suffering left out; leave it to them to talk in their histrionic and even hysterical way about "shattering this sorry scheme of things to bits and remolding it nearer to the heart's desire." If "man's chief end" is to be pleased and petted and made comfortable, then Omar Khayyam was right. But God has greater business in hand with you and me than that poor miserable ideal; and if the world were nearer to the heart's desire, it might be further from the soul's salvation. Do not think the trials and troubles are meaningless: one day you are going to look up into the face of God and thank Him for every sorrow, that drove its cruel ploughshare through your soul, and for every tear you ever shed.

> The cry of earth's anguish went up unto God,
>   "Lord, take away pain,
> The shadow that darkens the world Thou hast made,
>   The close-coiling chain
> That strangles the heart, the burden that weighs
>   On the wings that would soar.
> Lord, take away pain from the world Thou hast made
>   That it love Thee the more."
>
> Then answered the Lord to the world He had made,
>   "Shall I take away pain?
> And with it the power of the soul to endure
>   Made strong by the strain?
> Shall I take away pity that knits heart to heart
>   And sacrifice high?
> Will ye lose all your heroes who lift from the flame
>   White brows to the sky?
> Shall I take away love that redeems with a price
>   And smiles through the loss.
> Can ye spare from the lives that would climb unto mine
>   The Christ on His Cross?"

No, God knows best; and the true Christian reaction to suffering and sorrow is not the attitude of self-pity or fatalism or resentment: it is the spirit which takes life's difficulties as a God-given opportunity, and regards its troubles as a sacred trust, and wears the thorns as a crown.

Finally, let this be added—that the loveliest thing of all about the creative attitude towards suffering is that, if you are able to rise to it, not only do you develop your own character (for that might be a subtle form of spiritual egotism), but *you become a source of blessing and of strength to others.*

There is nothing on earth more beautiful to see than suffering transmuted into love. To say that the bitter cup can be drunk heroically is no more than every brave man knows already; but to say that one souls' hurt and suffering can distil out life and strength and healing for others—that is the everlasting miracle. But it happens. Do you remember how wonderfully it happened in the experience of John Bright? Richard Cobden called on his friend at Leamington one day and found him in the depths of grief and despair. "All that was left on earth," said Bright afterwards, describing that bitter hour, "all that was left of my young wife, except the memory of a sainted life and our all too brief happiness, was lying still and cold in the room above us." But "after a time Mr. Cobden looked up and said, 'There are thousands of homes at this moment where wives, mothers, and children are hungry. Now, when the first paroxysm of your grief is past, I would advise you to come with me, and we will never rest till the Corn Law is repealed!'" And so John Bright's desolating sorrow was transmuted into loving service of others. Is it not a blessed thing to know that your own sorrows, if you deal with them creatively, can be changed and transformed into a love that will lighten the burden of the sorrows of the world?

"If you deal with them creatively." "Yes," someone will say, "but that's just the difficulty. How am I to do it? I see now that suffering is not so much a problem to be explained, as a challenge to be met; but how am I to meet it? There's the rub. By what power am I to emerge as victor over every evil thing that threatens to defeat me? Unless you can tell me that, all you have been saying is left hanging in the air. It is true enough as far as it goes—but in the last resort it is not explanations I am wanting; it is power to 'stand in the evil day, and having done all, to stand' " (Ephesians 6:13).

I think you are right to make that demand. And I believe, to that quest, there is no answer except one. The only answer that can ultimately suffice is God Incarnate on a cross, facing there in His own person the very worst that suffering and evil have ever done upon the earth: Christ reigning from that deadly tree, confronting the powers of darkness at last with the startling discovery, that, what they in their pride had deemed to be a smashing and decisive blow against the empire of light and love, was destined to work out to their own undoing and disaster and to their final irrevocable defeat. For still He comes to us, this Christ victorious over all the mystery of suffering and evil, and offers to make His triumph ours.

That will be the theme of our next, concluding study—that cross of victory, "towering o'er the wrecks of time," shattering the chains of despair and oppression of spirit in which man has been bound captive by the tyranny of the mystery of evil, and flooding the darkest valleys of his earthly pilgrimage with the authentic light of heaven.

GOD AND THE FACT
OF SUFFERING

James S. Stewart (1896-   ) pastored three churches in Scotland before becoming professor of theology at the University of Edinburgh (1936) and then professor of New Testament (1946). But he is a professor who can preach, a scholar who can apply biblical truth to the needs of the common man, and a theologian who can make doctrine both practical and exciting. He has published several books of lectures and biblical studies, including *A Man in Christ* and *Heralds of God.* His two finest books of sermons are *The Gates of New Life* and *The Strong Name.* This sermon, and the three that follow, are all taken from *The Strong Name,* published in Edinburgh in 1940 by T. & T. Clark.

James S. Stewart

8

THE CROSS OF VICTORY

In all these things we are more than conquerors through him that loved us (Romans 8:37).

THERE WAS A day when Thackeray was walking out the Dean road to the west of Edinburgh, Scotland, with three companions; and as they went, they passed a quarry and saw, standing out against the sky above it, a great wooden crane—just like a cross. Whereupon Thackeray stopped, pointed, and murmured one word: "Calvary." Then they moved on, all suddenly grown silent and pondering deeply.

Why did Thackeray do that? Why should a novelist in the eighteen hundreds, and not a very spiritual one either, hark back instinctively to that death on the Judean hill long ago? Why should a Roman gallows, and the strange Man who hung there, haunt the imagination and the conscience of the race? How is it that we today, when the whole world is being shaken, are able without any sense of incongruity to sing:

> In the Cross of Christ I glory,
> Towering o'er the wrecks of Time?

It is because man, in the depths of his spirit, has always been conscious that there, in that cross, God has spoken, and eternity has intersected history. It is because we know that, past all our fumbling human attempts to answer the problem of evil and suffering, here is *God's* answer. Here, if anywhere, is the clue to solve the riddle.

Indeed, I doubt whether, apart from the cross, any of the other interpretations that we can find is ultimately of much avail. Think of the various beams of light in the darkness which we have already noticed. They are certainly there, shining through the midnight of our doubt and perplexity; real hints and indications of a purpose and a meaning behind the mystery. But leave out the cross, and will any of these lights, or all of them together, prove adequate in the hour of need?

Will it comfort a bereaved mother, grief-stricken by the death of a child, to be told about the beneficence of inexorable law, or the wisdom of the divine impartiality? These things may be true, as indeed they are; and a world in which these things are facts, even though it may sometimes involve tragedy for the individual, is undoubtedly—when you take a total view—a better and happier place than any world could be without them. But, will it meet that broken-hearted mother's need to go and tell her that? Will that make her "more than conqueror"? Or again, if you have a friend who is racked with fearful suffering, a martyr perhaps to rheumatoid arthritis, will you talk philosophically about the splendor of a dangerous universe and the providential purposes of pain? Or, if there is someone who has come through a shattering emotional crisis, some terrible dissappointment which has left life bleak and empty, will you go to that one and point out the creative function of trouble in producing character? Is that the best that you can do? Frankly, I should not like your task.

Difficulties in Accepting Suffering

Moreover, there are further difficulties. For instance, I can quite well imagine someone wanting to argue like this: "You say that suffering can make a positive contribution to life. You say it can bring enrichment to the soul. Well then, if that is so, why should we try to remove it? *If the thing brings blessing, why work for its abolition?* Better leave things as they are, and not meddle." Such an argument, it is clear, might become a dangerous opiate, lulling the human spirit into a false resignation and a pious acquiescence in all manner of evil things. Yet, the logic of the argument seems sound enough. Is this perhaps a place where logic breaks and goes to pieces on the facts of life?

Or, take this other difficulty which comes from a totally different direction. Even if we agree that God's aim is to produce character, and that in this realm there can be "no gains without pain," *we are still left with the question whether God could not have brought His sons and daughters to the same goal by some less tragic road.* It is not the fact of suffering that baffles us, for we can see that we need it; it is the frightful excess of the thing which seems so cruel and senseless and superfluous.

If God intends man's sanctification, why could He not have thought out some kindlier way? Surely it ought not to have been beyond the divine inventiveness to do that! Why should a man or a woman who is already a saint have to suffer fiendish agonies? If someone's whole world is wrecked by a tragic bereavement, or an accident which cripples for life, might not that one, hearing that these things are the price of character, cry out "It's not worth the price"? Or, if the nations go to war, if the cruelty of man brings a new cataclysm upon the earth and millions are driven into the valley of the shadow, it would be perfectly true to say that such suffering was the price of God's gift to man of the freedom of will; whereupon might not someone quite legitimately retort, "God's gifts at such a price are too dear—nothing is worth a price like that"? It is not suffering that is the mystery; it is the superfluity of it that baffles us. Leave out the cross—and will all the other beams of light in the darkness lead you very far?

There is still another difficulty. *We talk about suffering producing character. But it is perfectly obvious that it does not always have that effect.* It does not necessarily and inevitably sanctify. Sometimes its effect is the exact reverse. Sometimes it embitters. That gallant fighter, Robert Louis Stevenson, dying of incurable illness, cried, "Sick or well, I have had a splendid life!" There was a soul whom pain had ennobled. But, how different the reaction of John Keats in one of his low, peevish moods: "Lord!, a man should have the fine point of his soul taken off to become fit for this world." It is no use talking of the beneficent influence of pain, as though the thing worked automatically: it does not! Take this deeply significant confession, from Vera Brittain's *Testament of Youth,* describing the legacy of war:

"That's the worst sorrow," I decided, "it's always a vicious circle. It makes one tense and hard and disagreeable, and this means
that one repels and antagonizes people, and then they dislike and
avoid one—and that means more isolation and still more sorrow."

The fact is that in different lives, suffering produces
strangely different effects. One man loses his wife, and
the loss makes him far more tender and gentle. Another
faces the same loss, and it makes him hard and sullen.
One woman has a great sorrow, and it turns her to God.
Another passes through a similar experience, and she is
never seen inside a church again. It is all very well
talking about the blessed ministry of trouble; but it does
not always end in blessing. Paul declared, "All things
work together for good"; but he knew better than to leave
it at that. He never suggested that all things work
together for good invariably and unconditionally. He
said—"All things work together for good, *to them that love
God*" (Rom. 8:28). What we have to recognize is that
trouble, in itself, is neither positive nor negative: it is
neutral; whether it is going to become positive or negative
depends on the human reaction. Some, like that fine spirit
Katherine Mansfield, have the grace to use it creatively.
"I do not want to die," she wrote near the end, "without
leaving a record of my belief that suffering can be overcome. For I do believe it. Everything in life that we really
accept undergoes a change. So suffering becomes love."
That is the positive reaction: forcing trouble to yield up
its hidden, potential store of blessing. But we do not
always rise to that, do we, when trouble comes? "In all
these things we are"—what shall we say? "More than conquerors"? Would God it were true; but alas, how often
our negative reaction balks even His will to bless!

The Meaning of the Cross in Suffering

Now you see the crucial point we have reached.
Decisively, this fact emerges—that man's main concern
with the dark fact of suffering is not to find an explanation: it is to find a victory. It is not to elaborate a theory;
it is to lay hold upon a power. Even if you possessed the

answer to the riddle; even if you had it written down to the last detail and could say, "There is the full and final explanation of the problem of pain," that would not be enough, would it? For the pain itself would still have to be borne. That, in the last resort, is the real demand of the human spirit—not the explaining of this thing, but grace and help to bear it. *And that is why God gave us Christ.*

Open your New Testament. On every page of it you see the living God coming towards you, and He holds in His hands—not the ready-made answer to the vexed questions of the mind, but something better and diviner far: a liberating, reinforcing power for the soul! And this is why all the other beams of light converge at length upon a cross. Towering out of the dark it stands: God's everlasting answer to the quest of all the world.

See how the cross transforms the age-long mystery! What does it tell about the fact of suffering?

It tells you that *God is in it with you.* We are so apt to think of God as standing outside the sufferings of this world, apart and aloof in the untroubled serenity of heaven. "In this world," said Bacon, "God only and the angels may be spectators": and that is the implicit idea in many minds—a spectator God, dealing out pains and chastisements to His children, to see how they will react. But when I look with unveiled eyes upon the cross; when I grasp that the Sufferer hanging there is not just another martyr dying for his faith, but God incarnate, "love divine all loves excelling"; when I set that cross against the background of Christ's own tremendous word, "He that hath seen Me hath seen the Father"—then my heart makes answer to those who speak of a remote spectator God, "You are wrong! God is not outside the tears and tragedy of life. In every pang that rends the heart of man, woman, or little child, God has a share. In every dark valley of trouble and suffering, God is always present."

One of the most moving scenes in English literature comes at the end of Dickens' *Tale of Two Cities.* The carts were rumbling through the thronged streets of Paris to the guillotine. In one of them there were two prisoners:

a brave man who had once lost his soul but had found it again, and was now giving his life for a friend, and beside him a girl—little more than a child. She had seen him in the prison, and had observed the gentleness and courage of his face. "If I may ride with you," she had asked, thinking of that last dread journey, "will you let me hold your hand? I am not afraid, but I am little and weak, and it will give me more courage." So when they rode together now, her hand was in his; and even when they had reached the place of execution, there was no fear at all in her eyes. She looked at the quiet, composed face of the man beside her, and said, "I think you were sent to me by Heaven."

What is the Christian answer to the mystery of suffering? Not an explanation, but a reinforcing presence—Christ to stand beside you through the darkness, Christ's companionship to make the dark experience sacred. "Yea, though I walk through the valley of the shadow of death, I will fear no evil: for Thou art with me" (Psalm 23:4), and I think, Jesus, no, I know, you must have been sent to me by Heaven.

"Look!" rang out the cry in the Book of Daniel, "Did we not cast three men into the furnace? But now there are four! Who is that other? How come He is there, in the midst of the fire? Is it a spirit or an angel? What if it should be God? God walking there in the flame, to guard and save His own?" (Daniel 3:24-25, paraphrase).

How different suffering becomes to those who have seen that vision! It is not just that God knows, and sympathizes with you in your troubles, as any close friend might do. For He is so much closer than the closest friend. He is *in* you. And, therefore, your sufferings are His suffering, your sorrow His sorrow. Now that is true of all God's creatures. Just think what God's burden of suffering must be, when the pains of all the world are in His heart! No man who has once grasped this will ever again rail at Providence for being unkind. All our loud accusations and complainings are silenced and grow dumb before that vision of the immeasurable agony of God.

But remember this: if God is in it with you, sharing your suffering, it is also true that *you are in it with God, sharing His redemptive activity and His victory*. It is by the travail of the soul of Christ, by the age-long sufferings of God, that the world is moving on to its ultimate redemption. "With His stripes we are healed." Hence what suffering does, when it comes one day to you, is to give you a chance to co-operate with God. Every soul that takes its personal griefs and troubles and offers these up on the altar along-side the sacrifice of Jesus, is sharing constructively in that eternal passion of God by which all humanity shall at last find healing and peace. It is as though God said, in the day of darkness, "Here, my child, is something you can do for Me! Here is your little share in the burden which I have been carrying from the foundation the world and must carry until the day break and the shadows flee. Here is your part with Me in the age-long cross I bear." The man to whom that voice has spoken is trebly armed for the fight.

You must have noticed how often it happens that men and women who have met great tribulation in their own life come out of that experience with a wonderful new equipment for the service of God and their fellows. They reach the world's heart irresistibly, where others only grope and fumble. The real healers of the wounds of mankind are those whose own peace has been bought at a price; behind whose understanding and compassion and strong calm there lies some tale of Peniel, some deep, ineffaceable memory of a valley of shadow, a lonely way, and a grim wrestling in the dark. Mary Webb's lovely poem "A Factory of Peace" describes it well:

> I watched her in the loud and shadowy lanes
> Of life; and every face that passed her by
> Grew calmly restful, smiling quietly,
> As though she gave, for all their griefs and pains,
> Largesse of comfort, soft as summer rains,
> And balsam tinctured with tranquility.
> Yet in her own eyes dwelt an agony.
> "Oh, halcyon soul!" I cried, "what sorrow reigns
> In that calm heart which knows such ways to heal?"
> She said, "Where balms are made for human uses,

> Great furnace fires, and wheel on grinding wheel
> Must crush and purify the crude herb juices,
> And in some hearts the conflict cannot cease;
> They are the sick world's factories of peace."

If from one soul's hurt and conflict, the balm of healing and of peace can thus be distilled out for others; if pain can be transmuted into power; if, under Christ, our sacrifices can be taken up into His eternal sacrifice, and there can be made creative and redemptive—shall we still rail at life when it grows hard, and brood bitterly upon its cruelty and injustice? "Most gladly therefore will I rather glory in my infirmities, that the power of Christ may rest upon me" (2 Corinthians 12:9).

God is in it with you, and you are in it with God—that is the message of the cross on the mystery of suffering. And that message means victory. There was victory at the cross for Christ; and God wants you to know that there can be victory at every cross for you. Will you try, for a moment before we close, to focus the picture and get the crucified figure of the Christ right into the center of your thoughts? What do you see? It looks, at first glance, pathetically like defeat. It looks like the intolerable climax of all the pathos of the world. Here suffering and sorrow and the tragic element in life seem to blot out our fragile hopes forever. "O Sacred Head, sore wounded, with grief and shame weighed down!" But you do not see the cross aright at first glance. You have to gaze and gaze again. And those who do that make a marvellous discovery. They see, not Christ the pain-drenched Sufferer, but Christ the mighty Victor. They see the blackest tragedy of this earth becoming earth's most dazzling triumph. Their cry is no longer—"O broken, bleeding Victim, Thou mournful sacrifice!"—not that, but this: "O Jesus, King most wonderful, Thou Conqueror renowned!"

You have never truly begun to see the cross until you have seen that. Is there not a wonderful sense of mastery, right through the Passion narrative? Listen to His own words: "No man taketh [My life] from Me. I have power to lay it down, and I have power to take it again," (John 10:18). Is there not royalty in that? The irony of the situation was that Caiaphas, poor, blinded, self-deluded creature, thought that he held the reins and was the master-figure on the scene. "I have power to lay My life down," said Jesus. Is that defeat? See Him marching steadfastly to Jerusalem. Mark well His strong ineffable serenity through the last crowded, terrible days. Watch His bearing before Pilate. See Him on the cross refusing the drug they offered, that no atom of anguish should be evaded. Hark to the ringing shout that broke upon the darkness: "It is finished!" Is that defeat? Yes, it is; but not Christ's defeat—certainly not that! But the defeat of suffering. The defeat of the mystery of evil and of all the dark tragic powers of life—and Christ's victory! Thou art King of glory, O Christ—Thou Conqueror renowned!

"But what has all this to do with me?" you ask. "Christ may have conquered in the day of trouble, but my battle still has to be fought. Is there help in Calvary for me?"

Surely the answer is clear. If evil at its overwhelming worst has already been met and mastered, as in Jesus Christ it has; if God has got His hands on the baffling mystery of suffering in its direst, most defiant form, and turned its most awful triumph into uttermost, irrevocable defeat—if that in fact has happened, and on that scale, are you to say it cannot happen on the infinitely lesser scale of your own life, by union with Christ through faith? If you will but open the gateways of your nature to the invasion of Christ's Spirit, you will do as He did, and "lead captivity captive." "In all these things," wrote one who had tested the promise of God to the hilt in the worst tragedies of life, and therefore had a right to speak, "in all these things"—these desolating, heartbreaking things which happen to the sons of men; these physical pains; these mental agonies; these spiritual midnights of the soul—"we are more than conquerors," not through our own valor or stoic resolution, not through a creed or code or philosophy, but "through Him that loved us".

That is the only answer to the mystery of suffering, and the answer is a question—Will you let God in to reign? The answer is nto a theory. It is a life. It is a dedicated spirit, a fully surrendered soul. May that answer be ours!

Heaven's Help for Troubled Hearts

Walter A. Maier (1893-1950) was known
around the world as the speaker on "The
Lutheran Hour," heard over more than a thousand radio stations. Many of his faithful
listeners did not realize that this effective communicator was also professor of Old Testament
and Semitic Languages at Concordia Seminary
in St. Louis! It was said that Maier spent one
hour in preparation for each minute that he
spoke on the air. Numbers of his radio sermons were published in volumes still
treasured by those who appreciate good
preaching. This sermon is found in *For Christ
and Country,* published by Concordia
Publishing House, St. Louis, in 1942.

Walter A. Maier

9

HEAVEN'S HELP FOR TROUBLED HEARTS

Let not your heart be troubled; ye believe in God, believe also in Me. In My Father's house are many mansions; if it were not so, I would have told you. I go to prepare a place for you (John 14:1, 2)

AN EARLY MISSIONARY to Tierra del Fuego, the tip end of South America, tells us how every morning the natives of that barren country greeted the sunrise with piercing howls and shrieking lament. As he later learned in seeking an explanation for this weird rite, so much misery crowded into the lives of the Fuegians that they viewed each new day with horror, every sunrise as the beginning of added evil.

We are separated from Tierra del Fuego and those missionary days by 8,000 miles and many long years; yet, too many people in our country and this modern era, are gripped by the same fear which tortured those savages, likewise greet each dawn with grim forebodings. They have endured such unspeakable agony of body, mind, and soul; they have beheld so much misery on all sides, that each morning, instead of breaking with joyous hope, seems only to add grief to grief.

Men are asking themselves: "Where can we find unfailing comfort during crisis periods? In pleasure?" As late as Wednesday of this week, tea dances catered to large crowds in the Raffles Hotel at Singapore; people stood in long lines waiting to buy tickets for their favorite entertainment. Last night, Singapore fell. Can forgetfulness of sorrow be found in drunkenness? Positively not! The growth in liquor sales throughout the United States is so staggering that it ought to recall the prophet Nahum's warning concerning Nineveh, which was to be destroyed after drunken carousal. More than ever we need clear-thinking men and women whose perceptive powers have not been befuddled by overindulgence in alcohol.

Can money purchase release from fears and worries? Jay Gould, American multimillionaire, lamented on his deathbed, "I am the most miserable man on earth." Will unbelief, the denial of Christ, the overbrave reliance on self, conquer human miseries? Skeptical, sneering Voltaire cried out, "I wish I had never been born." Can courage be found in an alert, trained mind, the calmness of a pleasing personality? These advantages melt away quickly under the heat of affliction. In these days of trying men's souls, as promises prove unreliable, hopes misplaced, our own strength insufficient, we must turn penitently, pleadingly to God in Christ.

Whatever our individual troubles may be, let us find sustaining strength in faith! Through Christ we are in God's hand. For every perplixity, we can believe that in Jesus there is

Heaven's Help for Troubled Hearts

the comfort pledged by our Lord Himself in the words that have brought light and life to millions of sin-darkened souls. His radiant promise, is in John, chapter fourteen, verses one and two: "Let not your heart be troubled; ye believe in God, believe also in Me. In My Father's house are many mansions; if it were not so, I would have told you. I go to prepare a place for you."

In Christ We Have the Assurance of God's Help For This Life

Remove all doubt from your minds that there can be any exaggeration in these words! People are suspicious today. Again and again within this generation, they have been led to expect happier times with the blessings of peace, but throughout the world they face sorrows deeper than they have ever known. Diplomats break their word; politicians prove unreliable; scientists make bad guesses; prophets of new cults raise the hopes of their fellow men to the highest pitch, only to fail cruelly in producing real help. Yet this utterance of the Lord Jesus, as all His pledges, is divine truth, immovable, unchangeable, eternal. By His own declaration *"heaven and earth shall pass away, but My Word shall not pass away."* Christ's promise can never fail. Let that be our sustaining assurance! The Bible, as God's revelation, must prevail.

Our age particularly ought to be impressed with this sacredness of Holy Writ. Just a hundred years ago, in 1842, the first systematic excavations were undertaken in Bible lands, and the intervening period has indeed been a century of progress in defending Scripture. Archaeologists working in the ruins of ancient cities, especially in Assyria, Babylonia, Egypt, Palestine, have uncovered historical records, now three and four thousand years old, which remarkably support the Bible and corroborate its claims. Not, of course, that we need such human endorsement! Through the Holy Spirit the Christian knows God's Word is true; but how timely and helpful that, just in these days of brash unbelief, the promise has been fulfilled, "The stones shall cry out"! Therefore, when you face the cutting criticism of the Bible, remember how often those who had been the most bitter in assailing Christ's pledges, once they have really become acquainted with their truth, have defended the Scriptures.

George Romanes, the British biologist, wrote a book to support atheism. He explained, "I took it for granted that the Christian faith was played out." When, however, he saw that Christianity worked; that many eminent men, some the most illustrious in the fields of science, had ranged themselves on the side of the Gospel, he resolved to let the Bible speak for itself. As a result of his studies, he wrote a book called *Thoughts on Religion,* showing why, from the merely human viewpoint, everyone should be a Christian. He concluded—and now he speaks to you who have placed a question mark behind that statement of Holy Writ, "Unbelief is usually due to indolence, often to prejudice, and never a thing to be proud of."

"Let not your heart be troubled!" This word offers added comfort since it is among our Lord's final utterances,

spoken on the last night of His earthly life, shortly before He began the ordeal which was to end with His death on the cross. Jesus left His followers nothing of wealth or earthly value; but in this sacred pledge, He bequeathed them and us the heritage of untroubled hearts; and, within less than one day after speaking this promise, Jesus sealed it with His blood, died to prove its truth.

"Let not your heart be troubled!" Jesus says, for He recognizes the severe trials which burden our souls. Those who give counsel for the distressed often do not understand the problems they promise to solve; Christ knows our every sorrow. He was born in a stable and understands the needs of the poor and the outcasts. To save His life, He had to flee into a foreign country! He can measure the suffering of refugees, religious and political exiles. Jesus spent the greater part of His early existence in lowly work, and, more than any expert in labor or industry, He realizes what the laboring man requires. He suffered from hunger, thirst, weariness. Has anyone better insight into the privations to be endured by millions of the famished and undernourished? Christ was persecuted by those whom He had helped; and because He felt the pains of spurned devotion, He can sympathize with you who have been deserted by someone whom you loved and for whom you labored hard and long. He was slandered and defamed, although He was absolutely innocent of wrongdoing; and whenever false accusations blacken your character or baseless rumors disturb your peace, confide in Christ and know that He felt, though in a far deeper degree, the cruelty inflicted on you. What comfort, too, when faced with coaxing, tugging enticements for evil, to know that "He was in all points tempted like as we are" (Hebrews 4:15)! He was made to bear the unspeakable anguish of bodily suffering as the lash cut its furrow on His back, the blunt nails were hammered through His quivering flesh, and the tortures of crucifixion crushed out His life. When you toss on your sickbeds, broken by accident, consumed by wasting diseases, turn to Him for sympathetic love! He was burdened above all by inner agony in that un-

fathomable rack and torture of His soul when He cried, "My God, My God, why hast Thou forsaken Me?" (Mark 15:34). If it ever seems that God has left you; if you begin to doubt whether there is any salvation for your soul with its sins; if you verge closely to despair, then, what an understanding, compassionate Friend Jesus proves Himself to be!

Much more than sympathy, however, is found in Christ. He can say, *"Let not your heart be troubled,"* because He has removed forever the cause of fear and worry. Everything which disturbs your peace of mind, each affliction that has brought trouble into your home, every burden you must bear, is to be traced, finally but definitely, to sin, the transgression of which you or someone else is guilty. This war comes from sin. The tragedy in your home starts with selfishness. Your money losses originate in dishonesty and fraud. The sorrows you young people meet in courtship often begin with unfaithfulness and untruth. Even the sickness which lays us low, the injuries that seem to come merely by accident, are ultimately traceable to evil.

All glory to the Lord Jesus that He, Christ, forever broke the power of sin and completely removed its curse! Clinging to Him, we can exult, "Sin shall not have dominion over you: for ye are not under the Law, but under grace" (Romans 6:14). No dictator with the combined powers of Hitler, Mussolini, Stalin, and Franco, has ever exerted the complete sway over mankind and the full control over souls which mark the tyranny of sin. It locks us in its iron grip. You and I were born under its rule, and without Christ we die in its slavery. It burdens your conscience, robs you of your peace, and makes life a continued series of griefs, death and terrifying horror. Yet with Jesus—eternal praise to the compassionate Christ!— sin's curse has been removed from your life if only you will believe this divine assurance "He hath made Him to be sin for us, who knew no sin; that we might be made the righteousness of God in Him" (2 Corinthians 5:21).

How did Jesus remove your sins? Not by overlooking, forgetting, or simply canceling them, but by suffering for them, paying the price of every transgression, satisfying the demands of a just and holy God, giving Himself as the redemption for all iniquity, the sacrifice for the appalling total of human transgressions; by shedding His holy blood, the divine cleansing for each wrong; by laying down His life as the ransom price demanded for our liberation! You will not be able to understand how Christ could take away our sins. It is too miraculous, too marvelous, too merciful. Believe God and this promise of His Word, "There is therefore now no condemnation to them which are in Christ Jesus" (Romans 8:1)! When you give your heart to the Savior, your sins are removed *"as far as the East is from the West"*(Psalm 103:12). You are restored to grace, reconciled with God, and reborn into a new, blessed existence.

"Let not your heart be troubled!", Jesus assures you, because the same love that removes your sins can make the hardest blow the tenderest caresses, and use the galling bitterness of affliction for purposes of sweet, bounteous mercy. That is why a soldier leaving for distant fronts could write me, "It took this war to bring me to Christ." By the same love for your soul Jesus promises, not that you will escape trouble, that life will be a round of unbroken pleasure, but that through faith, "sorrow is turned into joy" as "all things work together for good to them that love God" (Job 41:22, Romans 8:28).

"Let not your heart be troubled!" This comfort is doubly sure because it comes not only from Jesus, who is our Christ, "the Lamb of God, which taketh away the sin of the world" (John 1:29), but also from Jesus, who is our God. Plainly He declares, "Ye believe in God; believe also in Me!" He asks men to trust Him as they trust the Almighty. What a powerful prooftext with which to confound those—and their number is increasing!—who are willing to pay our Lord almost every tribute except to admit that He is God, together with the Father and the Spirit, the everblessed Trinity! "Ye believe in God," He says; "believe also in Me!" for, as He states in John 10:30, "I and the Father are one." Jesus, according to His own words, according to Old Testament prophecies and New

Testament epistles, the proclamation of His Father, the adoration of the angels, the verdict of His miracles, is God almighty, with the resources of heaven itself at His command; God omniscient, who foresees the path we must take as the road to glory; God the ever present, whose pledge "Lo, I am with you always, even unto the end of the world" must be of outstanding consolation for millions subjected to the perils of war and its destruction; God all-merciful, to forgive us our selfishness and hatred, our impurities of thought and action, our rebellion against His grace, our refusal to help our fellow men. Jesus is all this, nothing less, yet much more. He is—hear it, believe it, trust it!—your God and your Savior.

The Lord who can help us, and whom this groping, bleeding age needs with double necessity, is the divine Christ. Tens of thousands of men have been nailed to crosses, though their suffering affects us little now. The day before yesterday 130 students at our seminary gave their blood, the largest single group of blood donors on record in this part of the country. While many lives may be saved by the transfusion of these gallons of vital life-fluid into broken, anemic bodies, all the human blood throughout the world can never cleanse a single sin-stained soul. Increasing numbers of American youth are laying down their lives in the nation's defense. God grant that their sacrifice will be rewarded by a true, righteous victory! But no man can give his life to pay for iniquity. Only God could do that; only God did do that when Jesus, our divine Savior, atoned for all sin.

Therefore, His appeal, "Ye believe in God; believe also in Me," is directed both to the young in the prime of hopeful lives, as they gird themselves for the service of war, and to the aged, who are passing the last milestones of life's long journey. "Believe . . . in Me!" He says to those who have placed their reliance on everything else except His grace—only to see their hopes completely shattered, "Believe . . . in Me!" He repeats to you who have found life easy and prosperous, but for whom the next years may bring sudden, complete reverses, "Believe . . . in Me!" He entreats those who have steadfastly spurned His outstretched arms, rejected every overture of His mercy, " 'Believe...in Me!' Accept Me as your Savior! Trust Me sincerely, perpetually, and your hearts will not be troubled!"

With faith in Christ, what can destroy your peace of mind, rob you of inner joy? Questions of money or of health, good name, quarrels in your home, losses in your business, matters of physical or mental health, the fear that your sons may never return from the battle lines? Listen to this promise: "If God be for us, who can be against us? He that spared not His own Son but delivered Him up for us all, how shall He not with Him also freely give us all things?" (Romans 8:31, 32). Whenever the burden seems too heavy, the way too steep, the night too dark, the pain too torturing, turn to Jesus! If He loved our souls so much that He gave His own body to rescue them for eternity, certainly He will take care of the comparatively small details of our earthly needs and use them for uplifting purposes.

Why are we so fainthearted, so reluctant to go all the way with the Savior? People in Saint Louis tell us of a traveler who in the early days came to the banks of the Mississippi during a hard winter, when the river was completely frozen over. Not trusting the strength of the ice, he began to crawl on hands and knees from the Illinois shore toward Missouri. Every advance was made slowly and cautiously. After covering a few hundred feet you can imagine his surprise when, hearing a loud noise behind him, he turned to see a wagon, loaded with heavy logs and drawn by two horses, move quickly over the frozen stream. In much the same way many of you are crawling on your knees, beset by worry and care, when, if you would only take God at His Word in Christ, you could walk safely across icebound rivers of doubt or affliction with the assurance of a blessed eternity constantly to strengthen you.

In Christ We Have The Pledge of God's Mansions For The Next Life

It is in this promise for the hereafter that the Savior's

grace reaches its glorious climax as it triumphs over the most fearful of terrors, death's paralysis. Men love life so dearly that they cringe in horror before the judgment beyond the grave and go to almost any extreme in avoiding the grim, clutching power of death. They will cling to rafts during thirst-crazed days and delirious nights; they will hastily throw away the earnings of a lifetime, if this weights them down in the race for safety; they will end raving, chattering, cursing in despair, as they see life slip from their grasp and know that before long they must face God. Add all other sorrows men endure, and their appalling total is not to be compared with the dread of the end! No scientific theories can offer any comfort here. No speculations, however learned, will dry tears at the side of a casket. No spiritist seances can ever remove the numb, aching pain of bereavement. Despite the systematic study of the circumstances surrounding thousands of deaths, science knows no more of the next life than did the ancient Egyptian pyramid architects or the Babylonian tower builders. The Bible is the only source of positive assurance regarding the hereafter, since it is the one Volume that offers God's revelation and Christ's assurance. If it were not for our Jesus and His divine comfort, *"Let not your hearts be troubled!"*, men would be cringing creatures, far worse, with this fear, than the dumb animals.

Through our Savior, however, we can exult: "O death, where is thy sting? O grave, where is thy victory?... Thanks be to God, which giveth us the victory through our Lord Jesus Christ!" (1 Corinthians 15:55, 57). See how clearly our Redeemer relieves death's pain! He tells His disciples in the Upper Room a few hours before He sets His face toward Gethsemane: "In My Father's house are many mansions...I go to prepare a place for you." He was going, first of all, to the cross; but beyond Calvary's shame and agony, He was directed to heaven. How overfilled are these words with personal comfort! He speaks intimately of His "Father's house," and He assures those who believe that there is a blessed existence for them after the grave. Cling closely to each word in this promise,

especially during these doubt-filled days when the
statements concluding the Apostles' Creed, "I believe. . .
in the resurrection of the body and the life everlasting,"
are assailed with new, destructive hatred or laughed at
in ridicule. We need a ban on every allegedly humorous
reference to heaven. Public or private slurs on Bible
teachings concerning the life to come are always objec-
tionable, but doubly so in an emergency like the present
when masses of American youth defending our country
may be close to death on land, in the air, and at sea. Men
by the millions are killed in world conflict, laid into hastily dug graves, their bodies drowned in the deep sea or
exposed to the devastating elements; and that, unbelief
sneeringly claims, is the end. How bitter and cruel life
would be if it were! Instead, we ought to find constant
comfort in the fact that, through Christ death is only the
beginning of glory incomparable, immeasurable, unutterable and unending.

One of our Lutheran families in Omaha had the har-
rowing experience of being informed soon after Pearl
Harbor that two sons, both volunteers, had been killed
aboard a battleship in Hawaiian waters. What anguish
must have shaken the souls of that father and mother,
even though their sons had died defending the nation!
Now, as you try to feel the heartbreaking sorrow of those
bereaved parents, you can begin to understand the
rejoicing which must have been theirs when recently they
received the electrifying report that the death notices
were mistakes, since the two boys had been found safe
and secure! Few people, I suppose, have ever thrilled with
such deep-souled rejoicing; yet everyone of you, my fellow
redeemed, accepting Christ's resurrection, His death-
destroying love for the world, can have the far greater
joy of knowing that, whenever unbelief says your dear
ones, asleep in Jesus, will never live again, this is a lie.
In God's good time you, too, will learn the full truth of
the Savior's pledge, "If a man keep My saying, he shall
never see death," (Romans 8:51), the eternal death. Here,
then, is the first promise Christ gives you today: The
grave does not end all. There is a future life, an eternity,

which the Lord of life Himself has won for us by removing our sins and destroying forever the power of eternal death.

We have only begun to survey the glories of His promise. Jesus also tells His disciples, and He includes all who receive Him as their Redeemer, that they shall be in His "Father's house," in heaven. What unspeakable bliss!—to be face to face with God the Father who gave us our existence; to sing our praises to God the Savior who redeemed us by His own life-giving atonement; to exalt God the Holy Spirit who gave us the new birth in holiness and righteousness—can any earthly privilege even approach this unspeakable joy?

Perfection, sinlessness, and absolute holiness always dwell with God. Therefore, the Scriptures want us to believe that in the celestial city we will experience no sorrow or grief, no pain or broken hopes, no partings or tears. There, in radiance we cannot describe or understand, all our frantic, unrewarded toils, the aching anguish of broken hearts, the sorrow of sin, will utterly vanish under the realization that "the sufferings of this present time are not worthy to be compared with the glory which shall be revealed in us" (Romans 8:18). Though we cannot even faintly picture its dazzling splendor, let us rest with the assurance that if this world, despite sin, contains marvels of breath-taking beauty—the towering mountains etched against the flaming sky, the amethyst-green surf, the ocean's fringe dashing restlessly on our shores, the rainbow arching its spectrum of color across the land—the celestial realm must be magnificent.

In His "Father's house," Jesus says, "are many mansions," a vast number of heavenly dwelling places. These everlasting homes will not remain empty; they have been reserved for the mighty host, the ten thousand times ten thousand, the myriad times myriads, who have been faithful unto death and have received the crown of life. You may be crowded out of many places on earth, but there is room for you in heaven. Jesus promises, "Where I am, there shall also My servant be" (John 12:26). Before the throne we shall meet those who have likewise died in the faith, the prophets and the apostles, the disciples and the evangelists, as well as those who "as a firebrand" have been "plucked out of the burning," rescued in the last moment, as the thief on the cross. Especially, however, will we be reunited with those Christians whom we knew in this life. Earthly relations like marriage will stop and give way to a higher, more blessed existence. For the comfort of those still wounded by recent bereavements, let me say the Scriptures contain no word which keeps us from believing that in heaven we shall be reassembled with those who have gone before us in the faith. What an incentive to remain true to Jesus! What a compelling reason for each member of the family to accept Him as your personal Savior!

Note the personal, pointed "I go to prepare a place for YOU." Jesus died for all the world, but I tell you individually that He gave Himelf for *you*. He shed His blood for *you*. He was crucified for *you*. He died for *you*. He rose again for *you*. Christ deals with the world through individuals; therefore *your* faith counts, not your church's, your parents', your wife's. *Your* name must be written in the Book of Life. How comforting in days like these when all else gives way to think of heaven not merely in a vague, indefinite sense, but as your "Father's house" with a spcial place prepared by Christ Himself for you!

"I" (Jesus) "go to prepare a place for you" helps answer the question "How can I be sure of my prepared place in the many mansions?" Some people try to earn their title to this heavenly dwelling, pay their way or have someone else pay it; pray themselves or be prayed into heaven. They want the blessings of the "Father's house" to be theirs in reward or recognition. But this is not Christ's teaching. He told His disciples on that Thursday night that *He,* as our Forerunner, our God and Savior, would make our place ready. How He fulfilled that promise and marked a celestial place with our names, what fearful price *He* paid to serve as our Way to heaven, is told in the story of Lent. May you learn to believe that by the shedding of His blood, His dying on the cross, His resurrection from the sealed grave, Jesus gives you, even now through faith, the indescribable blessings of eternity!

Why, then, with heaven as our real home, should our hearts be troubled! Why weep at funerals as those who have no hope? In the second century, a Greek named Aristides wrote to a friend concerning the early followers of our Lord: "If any among these Christians passes from this world, they rejoice and give thanks to God. And they escort his body with songs and thanksgivings, as if he were setting out from one place to another nearby." God grant you the same resolute faith, so that when death takes a beloved one or finally comes to summon you, you may rejoice in spirit, even though in tears of human sorrow! Clinging to the resurrected Christ, may you look forward joyfully to the "Father's house," with its "many mansions," the reunion with all God's children, and particularly to our own personal prepared place, where we shall behold our Savior. "For we shall see Him as He is." O God, bring us all to that glory for Jesus' sake! Amen.

The Heroism of Endurance

Hugh Black (1868-1953) was born and
trained in Scotland and ministered with
Alexander Whyte at Free St. George's in
Edinburgh. He served as professor of
Homiletics at Union Theological Seminary,
New York (1906-1938), and was widely
recognized as a capable preacher. This sermon
is taken from *Edinburgh Sermons* by Hugh
Black, published in 1906 by Hodder and
Stoughton, London.

Hugh Black

10

THE HEROISM OF ENDURANCE

If thou hast run with the footmen, and they have wearied thee, then how canst thou contend with horses? and if in the land of peace, thou wearies, then how wilt thou do in the swelling of Jordan? (Jeremiah 12:5).

THOUGH THE STORY of Jeremiah's life is fragmentary, we can read the story of his heart. Again and again we see something which reveals his inner nature. We see a timid shrinking man in process of hardening to make him the prophet required for his generation. That character, keen and strong like well-tempered steel, was formed in the fire. It was ever through the furnace of living pain. Of all the martyrdoms of the Bible—and it is a long record of martyrdoms—there is none so unrelieved as this one. Christ had keener sorrow, but He also had keener joy. He had a hope which was assurance. He knew that His blood would be the seed of the Church. Whatever the present might have been to Him, He had always the future. "For the joy that was set before Him He endured the cross, despising the shame" (Hebrews 12:2).

Jeremiah escaped pangs that only the pure heart of Christ could feel, but he was forced by the facts of his age to utter a message that had few notes of hope. He lived until he was an old man and saw the calamities he had himself predicted. His eyes, that had wept over the Holy City, saw it sacked and depopulated. He had to witness the fulfilment of his own words of doom. Unless we can enter with some sympathy into the sort of man Jeremiah was by nature, unless we can understand the man, we cannot understand the book. Once and again he wished to give up the task as too heavy a burden for him to bear; but always he was braced to face his destiny once more with clear eye and stern brow.

In the present instance, we see the prophet's education going on. We see him being hardened in the fire like a

Damascus blade. In a mood of depression, sick with his failure in the great city, he longs for the quiet village hallowed by the peaceful days of his youth. He turns to home like a tired bird to its nest, as a wounded beast drags himself to his lair—to find in the nest a scorpion! His fellow-townsmen, even his brethren and the house of his father, even they dealt treacherously with him. He is learning the *loneliness of life at the high altitudes.* The ordinary forms of good and evil easily find comradeship. Men shudder at an exceptional evil, and shrink from an exceptional good. Not everyone wants to breathe the foul vapors of the pit; not every one can breathe the rarefied air of the heights. Commonplace good and evil attract crowds according to their kind. Jeremiah had to pay the price of singularity. He had to learn not only to do without the sweet incense of popular favor, but also to stand unflinching, even when it turned into the hot breath of hatred. He had to submit, not only to be without friends, but to see friends become foes.

This experience through which the prophet passes is a cruel one. It either makes a man, or mars him, and nearly always hardens him. It creates an indignation, a holy anger sometimes against men, sometimes against the strange untoward state of affairs, sometimes against God. It has made some raise blasphemous voice and impious hand. Such an experience is always presented with the temptation, which came to Job, to curse God and die. The injustice of it rankles in the heart, unless the heart is bent humbly and inquiringly to God to learn what the true meaning of the visitation may be. Jeremiah here is kicking against the pricks which have wounded the feet of men for centuries—how to account for the fact that in a world governed by a righteous God, rightousness should often have to suffer so much. But in the midst of the cruel experience, he never lets go his grip of God. "Righteous art Thou, O God," he says—whatever comes, that is the first established fact of life. "Yet," he continues in holy boldness, "let me reason with Thee of Thy judgments. Wherefore doth the wicked prosper? Wherefore are all they at peace that deal treacherously?" His indignant soul, on fire for justice, cries out that it ought not to be so. But the undercurrent of the complaint is not the seeming prosperity of the wicked, but his own pain and sorrow and terrible adversity.

We do not ask a solution of the universe, until we are forced to ask a solution of our own place and lot in it. God's providence seemed perfect to Job, until he was caught in the tempest and tossed aside broken. We are not much concerned about mere abstract injustice. Jeremiah's *wherefore* about the wicked is really a *why* about himself? Why am I bared to the blast in following Thy will and performing Thy command? Why are tears and strife my portion? Why am I wearied out and left desolate, though I am fighting the Lord's battle? That is the prophet's real complaint.

Notice the answer, surely the strangest most inconsequent ever given. There is no attempt at explanation. *God never explains Himself in a ready-made fashion. God explains Himself through life. God explains Himself by deeds.*

The complaint here is answered by a counter-complaint. Jeremiah's charge against God, of injustice, is met by God's charge against Jeremiah, of weakness. "If thou hast run with the footmen, and they have wearied thee, then how canst thou contend with horses? If in the land of peace wherein thou trusted, then how wilt thou do [O faint-hearted one!] in the swelling of Jordan?" The "swelling of Jordan" means the dangerous ground by the river, where the heat is almost tropical and the vegetation is rank. It is a jungle, tangled bush where wild beasts lurk—leopards and wolves and (at that time also) lions. The answer to the complaint against the hardness of his lot is simply the assertion that it shall be harder still. He has only been running with footmen so far—he will have to contend with horses, and then he may have cause to speak of weariness. He has only been living in a land of peace so far—he will have to dwell in the jungle where there are wild beasts, and then he may talk of danger.

Does it seem an unfeeling answer? It was the answer Jeremiah needed. He needed to be braced, not pampered.

He is taught the need of endurance. It is a strange cure for cowardice, a strange remedy for weakness; yet, it is effective. It gives stiffening to the soul. The tear-stained face is lifted up calm once more. A new resolution creeps into the eye to prove worthy of the new responsibility. God appeals to the strength in Jeremiah, not to the weakness. By God's grace I will fight, and fighting fall if need be. By God's grace I will contend even with horses; and I will go to the swelling of Jordan, though the jungle growl and snarl. This was the result on Jeremiah, and it was the result required. Only a heroic soul could do the heroic work needed by Israel and by God, and it was the greatest heroism of all which was needed—the *heroism of endurance.*

Nothing worth doing can be done in this world without something of that iron resolution. It is the spirit which never knows defeat, which cannot be worn out, which has taken its stand and refuses to move. This is the 'patience' about which the Bible is full; not the sickly counterfeit which so often passes for patience, but the power to bear, to suffer, to sacrifice, to endure all things, to die, harder still sometimes to continue to live. The whole world teaches that patience. Life in her struggle with nature is lavish of her resources. She is willing to sacrifice anything for the bare maintenance of existence, meanwhile. Inch by inch, each advance has to be gained, fought for, paid for, kept. It is the lesson of all history also, both for the individual and for a body of men who have espoused any cause.

Christ's Church has survived through her power to endure. She was willing to give up anything to hold her ground, willing to pour out blood like water in order to take root. The mustard seed, planted with tears and watered with blood, stood the hazard of every storm, gripped tenaciously the soil, twining its roots round the rocks, reared its head a little higher, and spread out its branches a little fuller, and when the tempest came, held on for very life; and then, never hastening, never resting, went on in the divine task of growing; and, at last, became the greatest of trees, giving shelter to the birds of the air in its wide-spreading branches.

So is the kingdom of heaven. It is a true parable of the Church. She conquered violence, not by violence, but by virtue. She overcame force, not by force, but by patience. Her sons were ready to die—to die daily—to run with footmen, and then to contend with horses. It was given unto them not only to believe in Christ, but also to suffer for His sake (Philippians 1:29). They would not be stamped out. When their persecutors thought they were scattered like chaff, it turned out that they were scattered like seed. The omnipotent power of Rome was impotent before such resolution. The battle, not the barracks, is the place to make soldiers. The Church met the Empire and broke it, through the sheer power to endure. She was willing to suffer, and to suffer, and to suffer—and afterwards to conquer.

It is the same secret of success for the individual spiritual life. "In your patience ye shall win your souls." This method is utterly opposed to the world's method of enduring success, which is by self-assertion, aggressive action, force for force, blow for blow. Patience, not violence, is the Christian's safety. Even if all else be lost, it saves the soul, the true life. It gives fibre to the character. It purifies the heart, as gold in the furnace. "Violence does even justice unjustly," says Carlyle, which was a great admission for him, who worshipped might of any kind even when displayed in violence. The Church wearied out the Empire and then absorbed it. It was only when she forgot her Master's method and adopted the world's method, wielding the secular sword, that she grew weak. This is Christ's plan of campaign, for the Church and for the individual. "He that endureth to the end shall be saved" (Matthew 10:22).

What do we know of this heroic endurance? In our fight with temptation, in our warfare against all forms of evil, have we used our Master's watchword, and practiced our Master's scheme? Think of our temptation in the matter of foreign missions, for example. It is often looked on as a burden, something we must do because it has come to be expected as a sort of duty. It is not a fire in our bones which will give us no peace. It is not a task to which we feel we have been sent. We do not realize that Christ's soul is straightened until it be accomplished. We are easily made faint-hearted about it. We say that results are disproportionate to the effort; or rather (for that is not true) we are overpowered by the vastness of the work. If we find our small attempt a burden, how can we face the greater problem of God and His Christ? If we are wearied in our race with the footmen, how can we contend with horses?

We are so easily dispirited, not only in Christian enterprise, but also in personal Christian endeavor. We are so soon tempted to give up. The enemy is too hard to dislodge; a besetting sin in our lives is too stubborn; a rampant evil in our community is too deeply rooted; the beautiful kingdom of heaven of our dreams is an impossible task. Faint-hearted cravens that we are, what are we here in this world for? To find a land of peace in which to be secure? To look for a soft place? To find an easy task? To match ourselves against some halting footmen? We need some iron in our blood. We need to be braced for the conflict again. We need the noble scorn of consequence. What have we done, the best of us, for God or for man? What have we endured for the dream's sake? What have we given up in our self-indulgent life? What sacrifice have we ever made? The folly of beginning in the spirit, and at last ending miserably in the flesh! "Ye have not resisted unto blood fighting against sin" (Hebrews 12:4).

Is there to be no end to the warfare and the weariness? Is there to be no end in the individual struggle and in the social endeavor? Must Jeremiah harden himself forever and stiffen himself always to endure? Must we resist forever the sins of our own hearts? Must we protest forever against the evil of the world? *Forever,* if need be! To begin to serve God is to serve Him forever. It knows no cessation. Complainings die in His presence, and we are sent out again, Christ's belted knights—His forever.

If God sends a man to the pride of Jordan, it is well. He will not go alone. A land of peace without God is a terror. The jungle of Jordan with God is peace. Never a soul is tempted above what it can bear. Never a life is defeated that arms itself with the whole armor of God.

Lift up the hands which hang down, and strengthen the feeble knees, and make straight paths for your feet. "My grace is sufficient for you" (2 Corinthians 12:9).

The Ministry of Suffering

George W. Truett (1867-1944) pastored the
First Baptist Church, Dallas, Texas, from 1897
until his death, and saw it become the largest
Southern Baptist Church in the world. He was
a strong man with a tender heart, and undoubtedly he was one of the greatest preachers
of his time. A devoted denominational leader,
he served as president of the Southern Baptist
Convention and the Baptist World Alliance.
This sermon is taken from what I think is his
best book of sermons, *A Quest for Souls,*
published in 1917 and reprinted in 1928 by
Douglas, Doran & Company, Inc., New York.

George W. Truett

11

THE MINISTRY OF SUFFERING

Who is among you that feareth the Lord, that obeyeth the voice of His servant, that walketh in darkness, and hath no light? Let him trust in the name of the Lord, and stay upon his God (Isaiah 50:10).

THE BIBLE HAS a message for ever life, no matter what its duty or test or need. The vitality of the Bible is indestructible. No condition nor exigency of human life comes, but that the Bible has a word to meet it exactly. In every congregation such as this, there come some who have been called to walk the vale of suffering and sorrow and tears. Many people have paused at the close of a service to tell me of certain deep burdens they were bearing, or certain sore griefs that there were suffering, of certain deep perplexities that confronted them. I am to bring you a promise this morning—one of the most comforting and precious in the Bible. It is in the fiftieth chapter of Isaiah, the tenth verse, and you will keep it, because you will need this promise:

Who is among you that feareth the Lord, that obeyeth the voice of His servant, that walketh in darkness, and hath no light? Let him trust in the name of the Lord, and stay upon his God.

May I tell you how I came to find that promise? We are all along coming upon promises that we did not know were in the Bible. What a living book it is! And how increasingly wonderful it becomes, the more we read it and study it! I was in one of the Texas cities some years ago, preaching in some daily meetings, and my attention was called to the devotion to Christ of a noble mother in that congregation. I had rarely seen anything to rank with her devotion. Some months went by, and there came from that city to my city, another mother from that church, and presently I asked her about the first mother. She said: "I came especially to see you about the first mother. Her case is unspeakably pitiful. It is this: She has come to the place, because of trouble, sorrow and suffering, where her spirit seems all beaten into the dust, and she is without light. If you ask her the question if she trusts Christ, she will answer, without hesitation, in the words of Job: 'Though He slay me, yet I will trust Him.' "But," said the second mother, "this first mother is in deep darkness and is without light. I have come to you to ask if there is some suggestion you can give her out of God's Word." That is how I came to find this text.

Now you are ready to hear it quoted again. Mark it, for you will need it: "Who is among you that feareth the Lord, that obeyeth the voice of His servant, that walketh in darkness, and hath no light? Let him trust in the name of the Lord, and stay upon his God." "Who is among you that feareth the Lord,"—the fear of the Lord is the beginning of wisdom—"that obeyeth the voice of His servant, that walketh in darkness, and hath no light?" That was her case, exactly. What is to be done? The rest of the verse tells us: "Let him trust in the name of the Lord, and stay upon his God."

You will be glad to know, to trace the story just a moment further, that this promise was the message God used to recover this bedarkened, sorrowing mother and to thrill her heart again with glorious peace.

Let us look at that promise a little while, because sooner or later all our feet must go down that vale of sorrow and suffering and darkness and tears, and this text describes a condition that will sometime come to us all. What is the condition? Here is one that fears the Lord and obeys the voice of His servant, and yet walketh in darkness and hath no light. That is the condition that sometimes comes to us in our earthly experience; and that condition is sometimes the severest test that ever comes to us. Darkness is always trying to us. Darkness is trying to us physically, especially when we are ill, and agitated, and disturbed. Oh, how sick people dread the night and long for the morning! Surely, they will be better when the light comes! And when we come into the realm of religious darkness, how terrible such darkness becomes, and how glorious is light when it streams down on our darkness!

It raises an old question, as old as Job, and it may be older: Why do tears, sufferings, and darkness come to those who are the friends of God? We can understand why trouble would come to the man who is not God's friend and refuses to be, for as a man sows, so shall he reap. If he sows to unbelief, the reaping must be of a godless man, the man who will not be God's friend at all, would come to the harvest of distress. We can understand that. But that is not the difficult question. The question is: Why do sufferings, darkness, and tears come to those who are the friends of God?

Now, sometimes there is an off-hand, superficial answer given at that point. Sometimes when a Christian is seen to be in darkness, trouble, and tears, the superficial critic pounces upon him and says: "This trouble comes as the result of some sin." The Word of God is not that cruel. The Word of God does not teach that doctrine. That doctrine is as false as it is cruel, and as cruel as it is false. When you turn to the Word of God, it is perfectly clear. Listen:

> For whom the Lord loveth He chasteneth, and scourgeth every son whom He receiveth . . . If ye be without chastisement . . . then are ye bastards, and not sons. Furthermore, we have had fathers of our flesh which corrected us, and we gave them reverence; shall we not much rather be in subjection unto the Father of spirits, and live? (Hebrews 12:6-9).

And then the beautiful words of Jesus are in point just here, where He says: "As many as I love, I rebuke and chasten" (Revelation 3:19). So you see, a part of the program and plan and experience of human life is chastisement, is trial. "In the world," said Jesus, "ye shall have tribulation." It is one of the most expressive words in the Bible. But He goes on to say: "But be of good cheer; I have overcome the world" (John 16:33).

But now, we are raising the question: Why do the friends of God pass down the vale of suffering, darkness, and tears? There are some partial answers to which our attention may be called. I say partial answers. They must be partial. The full-orbed and complete answer we must wait for, until we shall read it yonder in the golden glow of the land and life above. But, there are partial answers why trouble, trials, tears, darkness, and suffering come again and again to the friends of God here in this world. Let us glance at some of these partial answers.

Suffering Enables One to Honor God

For one thing, *trouble, if rightly used, enables us to honor God.* Trouble, then, is a *trust,* and we are thus to receive it. We understand about other things being trusts. There is the man of education; he must answer for those superior attainments. There is the one who can sing so the hearts are enchanted by the music; that singer must answer for that gift. There is the man of money, and the man of money must answer for it. The men who make money must answer for that capacity. Whatever our gifts or capacities, all of them are to be received as trusts from God, to be used in His name, to help humanity. Now, along with other trusts comes trouble. Trouble is to be received, however it comes, as a trust; and we are to bear it, we are to meet it, we are to go through it, we are to face it like we ought, as a trust from God, to be used for the glory of His great name.

You recall Job's manifold and fiery trials, that patriarch in the land of Uz, that conquering business man, and that faithful friend of God—Job, the man whom God so approved and applauded. One day Satan impiously said to God: "If you will give me a chance at your man Job, I will shake his religion out of him, and I will make him deny you." Said Satan impiously to God: "Your man Job is serving you because of sheer selfishness. He knows, in the crude saying of the world, 'which side of his bread is buttered,' and, therefore, is he proposing to serve you. Give me a chance," said Satan, "and I will make him deny you." And God said to Satan: "I will give you carte blanche at Job. You may do anything you please to him except to kill him." And then, the awful testing began.

There was Job, all unacquainted with the colloquy between Satan and God, happy and prosperous in all his surroundings. And then, there came a dark-robed messenger, which took from him all his property; and I tell you, when you strike a man in his property; you have dealt him a staggering blow; and some men seem never to recover from such blows. What a pity that it is so! Then there came another messenger, saying that this trouble had come to Job—his servants were all taken away; and then there came another messenger, telling him the awful tidings that his children, all and each, had gone down into dusty death. But stricken and beaten to the very dust though that father was, he simply made answer through the darkness: "The Lord gave, and the Lord hath taken away. Blessed be the name of the Lord" (Job 1:21).

Then there came another black-robed messenger, and Job was stricken in his health; so that from the crown on his head to the soles of his feet, his body was one festering mass of affliction and suffering. And when his former friends in the days of his prosperity came to see him, so grievous were Job's sufferings, that those men sat around him for seven days and did not deign to open their lips, so terrible was Job's plight. And when at last they did speak, they said, in effect: "Job, you are the worst man out of perdition, or this never would have come to you." Miserable comforters were they all! Job said to them: "Gentlemen, your diagnosis is incorrect. I do not know why the awful aggregation of troubles has come down to swallow me up, but let come upon me what will; though He slay me, yet I will trust in Him." And God brought Job out of all those troubles and made the latter days of his life incomparably more glorious than the former. Today you and I are strengthened by the very recitation of how God sustained Job in the black Friday that long ago came to his life.

There was a time in my life, when, for days and days, the only book I wanted to read was the book of Job. I read it through and through and through—that book of Job, that tells how the human heart is swept in its deepest depths of suffering and darkness, and yet how God blesses it and brings it up and out and sets the soul again in the high place of safety and peace. *Trouble rightly borne honors God.* Be careful, when trouble comes, how you behave. No matter what the trouble is, no matter how it came about, God is dishonored, if a Christian does not bear his fiery trial like he ought to bear it. You are being tested for God; and you will dishonor Him outrageously, or you will honor Him gloriously, according to your behavior when trouble is on. Remember that.

I am thinking now of a Christian girl who married a noisy, disputatious unbeliever. Serious matter that is. Oh, when will people as seriously view this destiny-shaping question of marriage as it ought to be viewed? When will parents be as careful in their teaching about it, and young people as careful in their decisions about it, as they ought to be? This dear girl, a glorious Christian, was wooed and won by a handsome young fellow, but he was a scorner of the things of God; and she went into that atmosphere. His father and mother and his grandparents were likewise stout unbelievers, and all of them lived in the same big home. And then there began a daily trial of that girl's faith. The most insidious attacks were made on her faith, from this angle and that, but she held calm and steadfast and true to Jesus during all of that first year of their wedded life. She had to make her way to the house of God alone, but she went to worship. That went on for about a year.

One day, as she moved about the duties of the kitchen, her clothing caught fire, and before they could reach her and put out the fire, she had received burns from which she died, a few hours later. But while she lived, she was conscious to the last, and she bore her sufferings with all the glorious devotion of some mighty martyr for God. Never a word of reproach or bitterness escaped her lips— never one word. She went on quoting God's great and precious promises to the last; and when it was evident to her that she was going, she stretched out those charred, blackened, once beautiful hands and arms, and tried to put them around her husband's neck, and said: "Poor Charlie, the thing that tries me, and the only thing, about going away, is that I have not lived long enough to teach you and your dear parents and the dear old grandparents, that Jesus is real and sure, that He is a Savior, That He does help us, and that He is our refuge in every time of trouble and need." And then she went away, the funeral was held, and the body was left to rest in the cemetery. The family returned to the home, the day died down to nightfall, and there by the open fire sat the bereaved ones, when presently the young husband stirred and said to his father and to his grandfather: "Mary had what the rest of us do not have, and I am going to seek her Savior." And the father said: "My boy, you are right. I know it. I feel it. She has taught me that, and I will seek Him, too." And the old grandfather stirred, put his staff out, came over to the son and grandson, laid his hand on the head of each, and said: "My sons, you are right. Mary did have what the rest of us do not have, and I am going to seek her Savior, too." And in three days all those men had found Christ, as did also numbers of their loved ones around them. A little woman, called to pass through the vale of deepest darkness and suffering, honored God through it all, and her testimony was irresistible. Be careful how you behave when trouble is on you! If you carp, cavil, criticise, murmur, and are evil in your speech, oh, how you will dishonor God! Trouble rightly borne will surely honor God.

Suffering Allows God to Bestow His Grace

Why do darkness and sufferings and tears come to God's people? There is another partial answer. *They furnish an occasion for God to bestow His grace.* If I may so put it, they give God a platform on which to stand and do His great work. For example, there is a lawyer, well trained in the schools, and he has received his diploma and is ready for his noble calling. Now, if he is to evince his skill in legal learning, he must have his case. Yonder is a doctor who had been graduated after years of painstaking study. If that doctor is to demonstrate his skill in medicine, he must have his case. Even so, the Lord Jesus Christ, if He is to show men what He can do for them, in the black Fridays, in the darkest vale, in the most dreadful hour, then the hour of trouble and darkness must come; that He may come and extricate us therefrom.

How often is that truth illustrated! Paul had his thorn

in the flesh. I do not know what it was, but it was something serious, you may be sure. He called it the messenger of Satan, sent to buffet him, and thrice Paul besought the Lord to take away that thorn in the flesh; but it was not taken away, and after that, Paul said: "I am glad I have it. I glory in it, because God has given me more of His grace than I ever would have had, but for the thorn, and so I will take the thorn and the added grace and be enlarged in my knowledge and experience of God."

Suffering Prepares One to Help Others

Why does trouble come to the child of God? *Many a time, it is the strange way of preparing such friend of God to be a helper of others, as such person otherwise never could have been.* There is no teacher like experience. I wonder if we really and deeply learn anything at all, except as we learn it in the realm of experience. And so trouble often comes and as we pass through it, we are fitted to be helpers as we never could have been but for such trouble. Paul discusses that particular doctrine when he says: "God comforteth us in all our tribulations, that we may be able to comfort them who are in any trouble, by the comfort wherewith we ourselves are comforted of God" (2 Corinthians 1:4).

I am thinking now of two young mothers. The baby of the first one died after a brief illness, maybe a day and night, and I was summoned to the funeral. She and the husband were not Christians. They were quite worldly and quite godless, so I had a difficult time, indeed, in reaching them and speaking to them. I went with them, in their brokenness and desolation, to the cemetery and came back with them. I said to them: "You will come to God's house, and you will get comfort there." And so they came; and in a few Sundays both of them came into the light and were saved. They took their place in the church and became faithful followers of Jesus. Months went by, and one day I was summoned to another funeral. The second little mother was called to put away her flaxen-haired little girl. She was utterly despairing and desolate in her grief. She, too, was an unbeliever. I read the sweetest Scriptures I could find to help her, but she did not seem to hear a word I said. At last, as the quartette began to sing, the first young mother I have described came quietly from the place where she was, took her place beside the second mother, put her arms about her, and gently said: "Oh, Jennie, dear, it is going to be all right!" And Jennie answered back: "Why, Mary, it cannot be all right! Everything about it is bad, dark and wrong.! It cannot be all right!" "But," said the first mother, "I passed through this; I know what you are going through. God called me, and through the darkness I came to Him. He has comforted me, and He will comfort you, Jennie, dear. You cling to Him and He will bring you out." And the first mother did more for the second mother than I could have done, maybe in days and months, for the first little mother had traveled that road of suffering herself. Oh, it is often that way, my friends! The world's highest blessings often come out of its deepest sorrows, trials, and tears. Heaven itself can be entered only by way of the cross. There is no way to get there except by the cross of Christ.

Did you ever read J.M. Barrie's charming little book, *Margaret Ogilvy?* Everyone should read it. There is one chapter in it on "How My Mother Got Her Soft Face." The author is really talking about his own mother. The story is that the oldest son in the family went away from home when he became of age—went out to the big world to fight the battle of life for himself. Letters came and went, through the months of separation, between the son and his mother. One day a wire came to her that the son was desperately ill, and she had better come at once. She hurriedly packed her valise and started to the railroad station, some miles away, committing the tasks of the home to the younger children to do the best they could with them; but before she reached the station, there came a second messenger boy with the telegram, notifying her that her boy had died and his body was being sent home on the next train. Following the funeral, the mother moved about the house, her face betokening a sorrow too deep for human speech. But after some weeks, they saw her face shone with a light that was never on land or sea. Not a murmur escaped her, no bitterness, no complaints, no harsh words; hers was a patience like unto Christ's patience. And when some neighboring woman lost her boy or her girl, when sorrow came to a neighboring home, Mr. Barrie said, five miles away, ten miles away, twenty miles away, forty miles away, the suffering and sorrowing one said: "Send for that woman who has the soft face. She will know what to say to us, for she has passed down the valley of suffering herself." Oh, my friends, suffering is often the way whereby we are fitted to help a broken, bruised, sinning, suffering world, as we never otherwise could help it!

Suffering Helps Build Character

Why do sufferings and tears come to us? There is another word. Many a time, *it is necessary discipline for us in the building of our own character.* Mark you, God's great concern is for our character—for what we are, not what we seem to be. God's great concern is for our inner deeper selves. Again and again, trouble is God's disciplinary teacher to give us that experience that shall refine us, teach us, cleanse us, and fit us, that we may be and do in God's sight what He desires. The highest conception of life here is that it is a school; you and I are the pupils at school, and God has many teachers. One of His teachers that comes robed in black is suffering, is trial, is deepest, darkest testing. David said: "It is good for me that I have been afflicted, that I might learn thy statutes" (Psalm 119:71). Oh, we need, my friends, to be disenchanted! Ease is the bane of everything that is good. We need to be disenchanted, so that our trust shall not be in the flesh, nor in the world, but stayed on the living God.

I am thinking now of a little woman who was happily married. Two children were given her; she lost both of those children, and they were buried in the same grave.

Then she came down with a complete, nervous collapse; and for some years, she was as helpless as a little child. She had to be fed by loved ones, who ministered to her. One day, as her aunt, who was a joyful Christian, was feeding this little, helpless woman, who was unusually despondent on that particular morning, the little woman said: "Oh, auntie, you say that God loves us. You say it, and you keep saying it. Oh, auntie, I used to think He did, but, auntie, if He loves us, why, *why did He make me as I am?"* And her wise aunt, after kissing her gently, waited a moment and said: *"He has not made you yet, my child. He is making you now!"*

> When, through the deep waters I call thee to go,
> The rivers of sorrow shall not overflow,
> For I will be with thee, thy troubles to bless,
> And sanctify to thee thy deepest distress.
>
> When through fiery trials, thy pathway shall lie,
> My grace, all-sufficient, shall be thy supply,
> The flame shall not hurt thee—I only design,
> Thy dross to consume, and thy gold to refine.

Suffering Encourages One to Trust God

There is one word more. What are we to do when the trouble is on? Isaiah 50:10 tells us. "Who is among you that feareth the Lord, that obeyeth the voice of His servant, that walketh in darkness, and hath no light?" What is that one to do? Here it is: *"Let him trust in the name of the Lord, and stay upon his God."* There is your anchor. It is not anywhere else. You will grope and flounder and be in the ditch anywhere else, my friends. Some of you have been called to pass through deep troubles—fiery troubles. You will fatally err if you go anywhere else but to God. There is your anchor. If you have an anchor for a ship, you do not keep the anchor in the ship when you need to anchor the ship. You take the anchor and let it down. So our anchor is not within us at all. We are anchored to Christ. Listen to His promises: "Because I live ye shall live also." And again: "I will never leave thee, nor forsake thee." And again: "And, lo, I am with you always, even unto the end of the world." That anchor will hold. And if you do not stay upon God in the dark and trying day, you have serious cause to suspect whether you have ever really trusted Him at all. Trust Him in the dark day, because God's grace and promises are designed for dark days, just as those great ships are built yonder to withstand the stoutest storm that ever drives the seas. Why should you trust God on the dark and cloudy day? Because such a faith will glorify God. With your submission to God's will—patient, meek, and uncomplaining;—with your clinging trust, like Job, saying, "I will trust Him, though He slay me," saying, "Whatever comes, I will follow Him the best I can, whatever the vale through which I walk"—if you will trust Him like that, you shall be a blessed witness for God.

Why are you to trust Him on the dark and cloudy day? Because it will not always stay dark and cloudy, thank God! Sure are His promises that "the day will break and the shadows flee away." "Weeping may endure for a night, but joy cometh in the morning." "For our light affliction, which is but for a moment, worketh for us a far more exceeding and eternal weight of glory" (Psalm 30:15; 2 Corinthians 4:17). It will not stay dark. There comes a sweet, fair morning, tinted and glinted with all the favor of God; and you are to look forward to that morning, cling to Him, and go your way, knowing that all shall be well.

Tell me, was this message for somebody today? Oh, receive it and follow it! Is some heart perplexed and darkened? Take the text, I pray you, and go with it, making it your own. Take one step at a time, and then take another step, and then take another step, and He will bring you into the fair day, and you will sing with the poet:

> So I go on, not knowing;
>   I would not know if I might.
> I would rather walk with Christ in the dark
>   Than to walk alone in the light.
> I would rather walk with Him by faith
>   Than to walk by myself with sight.

Stay yourself upon Him today and from this day forward

cleave ever to Him with unhesitating trust, and then you may sing with the psalmist, that the Lord will perfect that which concerneth us, because His mercy endureth forever.

The Problem of Pain

George H. Morrison (1866-1928) assisted
the great Alexander Whyte in Edinburgh,
pastored two churches, and then became
pastor in 1902 of the distinguished Wellington
Church on University Avenue in Glasgow. His
preaching drew great crowds; in fact, people
had to queue up an hour before the services to
be sure to get seats in the large auditorium.
Morrison is a master of imagination in
preaching, yet his messages are solidly
biblical. From his many published volumes of
sermons, I have chosen this message, found in
The Afterglow of God, published in 1912 by
Hodder and Stoughton, London.

George H. Morrison

12

THE PROBLEM OF PAIN

Neither shall there be any more pain (Revelation 21:4).

THIS, AS YOU all know, is Hospital Sunday, when offerings are received for our local hospitals. It is that fact which I have had in view in choosing my subject. I have already spoken on the doctrine of the body, for it is with the body that medical science deals; not with the body, however, in a state of health, but with the body in a state of pain and sickness; and so I thought I would take this opportunity to speak on the problem of pain, a theme that reaches home to everyone. Now, please remember at the very outset that at the best I can only make suggestions. I am not so foolish as to imagine that I can settle this problem. I can only give you certain points of view, some thoughts that may flash a little light upon the darkness; but, at least, I can truly say that I shall give you nothing that has not come with comfort to myself.

Now the problem of pain, I think I may assert, is in its full intensity a modern problem. There is today a sensitiveness to pain which in past ages was unknown. When you go back three or four centuries, you read of the most excruciating tortures. And you say how cruel must men have been in those days, when they could actually use these frightful instruments. Well, of course, there was much cruelty about it, but remember there was also a certain callousness—an absence of that quivering sensibility which makes us shrink from suffering today. Still more conspicuously was this the case in the ancient world of Greece and Rome. It was a cruel and a callous world. It was not alive to the mystery of pain. Even the author of the Book of Job, which deals with suffering, is not perplexed about the fact of suffering. It is the question why the *righteous* suffer that forms the burden of the Book of Job. The problem, then, is largely a modern one. It has become insistent in these latter days. Is it possible,

do you think, to find the reasons that may have led to
this emergence? Why, in other words, are we today more
sensitive to pain than were men of years ago? Why do
we dwell on it more, and feel its pressure more, than men
seem to have done in the old world? Let me suggest to
you three reasons that may help to account for that new
sensibility.

The Pressure of Pain

In the first place, *the keener sensitiveness to pain springs
partly from our new power of escaping it.* The fact that
we can so often cheat it now has had the effect of calling
attention to it. So long as anything is quite inevitable,
we grimly and silently accept it. *Death* is inevitable—no
man can escape it—and yet you and I seldom think of
death. But just suppose that someone were to come and
tell us a secret for escaping death, would not the fact of
death leap into prominence? So it is with the fact of pain.
Men thought that pain was inevitable once. There it was,
and one just had to bear it, and that was the end of the
whole matter. But now, thanks to the discoveries of
science, and to the wonderful appliances of Christian
medicine, we look on pain in quite a different light. A
doctor will actually come to you and say, "It is your duty
not to suffer." I had a first-rate doctor who once said to
me, "You have no right to suffer pain like that." And it
is just this sense that pain is not inevitable, but may be
relieved and avoided somehow, that has helped to call attention to its problem.

A second reason for the pressure of the problem is to
be found in *the new sense of the solidarity of life.* We feel
our kinship now with all creation in a way that was un-
dreamed of once. Men, of course, have always recognized
that there was kinship between them and the dumb
animals. But, in bygone times, it was not of *that* they
thought; it was rather of the *chasm* between man and
beast. Now, thanks to the knowledge we have won, it is
not on the chasm that thought is centered. It is on the
wonderful closeness of the ties that link all living things

into a unity. Now, the moment you have built that bridge, there comes galloping over it the form of pain. Pain is universal in the world; wherever there is life, there is suffering. And it is the new sense which we have gained of the suffering throughout the animate creation that has given to the matter a new prominence. You know how John Stuart Mill has dwelt on that. You know how Huxley has dwelt on that. They have taken the pain of bird, beast, and fish, and flung it in the very face of God. And what I say is that that new conception of the groaning and travailing of all creation helps to explain the pressure of the problem.

But there is another reason, it seems to me. It is not scientific; it is theological. *It is the discovery we have made in these last days of the full humanity of Jesus.* Can you detect the bearings of that upon the question? Let me try in a sentence to explain it to you. Well, so long as the faith was viewed as a body of doctrine, so long there was little room in it for pain. It was *with sin* it reached the love of God. But, the moment that out of the mist of ages there stepped the figure of the man Christ Jesus, in that moment there flashed upon the world the recognition of the fact of pain.

Here was the Christ, the very Son of God, and He was infinitely sensitive to pain. It was His passion to cure it when he met with it. For Him it was a terrible reality. And I suggest that it is the human Christ who has become so real to us today who has made real to a thousand hearts the problem of our human suffering. Men are not deeply interested, perhaps, in dogma now; but they are deeply interested in Christ Jesus. They want to look at the world through Jesus' eyes in a way that was never thought of in past ages. And I think that when you get that standpoint, immediately, as in the days of Galilee, you are confronted not alone with sin, but also with the terrible spectacle of pain.

The Place of Pain

Now, to show you the place that pain has in our being,

there are some *facts* I want to bring before you. And the *first* is that our *capacity for pain is greater than our capacity for joy*. You experience, for instance, a great joy. Does that prolong its sway through the long months? Do you not know how it exhausts itself, and dies, as Shakespeare says, in its own too much? But now you experience great pain, and I never heard that *that* must needs exhaust itself—it may continue with a man for years. That means that our capacity for pain is deeper than our capacity for joy. It means that we are so fashioned by the infinite, that the undertone of life is one of sorrow. And I mention that to show you how our nature, when you come to understand it in the deeps, is in unison with the message of the cross.

Another *fact* which we shall pick up as we pass is this, that *pain is at the root of life and growth*. It is not through its pleasures, but through its pains, that the world is carried to the higher levels. You remember how Burns wrote about our pleasures?

> But pleasures are like poppies spread,
> You seize the flow'r, its blossom is shed.

and that is not only true of men; it is true also of the progress of the world. It is through suffering that we are born, and it is through suffering that we are fed. It is through agony that we have won our property; it is through blood that we have reached our freedom. It is through pain—pain infinite and unutterable, the pain which was endured by Christ on Calvary—that you and I are ransomed and redeemed. Now that is a fact; explain it how you will, and we are here to deal with facts. I do not deny that pain may be a curse—remember that it also is a power. We owe our laws to it, and all our art. We owe to it our immortal books and our salvation. We owe to it the fact that we are here and able to look the problem in the face.

The *third* fact I note is to me of the deepest significance. It is *the tendency which men have always had to think of pain as acceptable to God*. We talk of the duty of happiness till folk are almost tired of hearing of it. Now, not for a single moment would I question that it *is* our bounden duty to be happy.

But, how significant and singular it is that in every country and in every age men should have looked on suffering and pain as something that was acceptable to God. You have it in the Roman knight who, to appease the gods, leaped into the chasm. You have it in the Indian fakir who sits for years in an attitude of misery. You have it in the pilgrim to the shrine; in the hermit and in the lonely anchorite; in every saint who ever scourged himself; in every savage who has made his offering. Whatever else that means (and it means much else), it hints at something mysterious in pain. Men feel instinctively that in the bearing of it there is some hope of fellowship with heaven. You may despise the hermit, and you may flout the saint when the weals are red upon his back, but an instinct which is universal is something you do well not to despise.

The Purifying Power of Pain

That leads me to touch, just for a moment, upon the purifying power of pain, for that is more closely akin than we might think to the feeling that it pleases God. Now I am far from saying that pain *always* purifies. We have all known cases where it has not done so. We have known men who were hardened and embittered by the cup of suffering they had to drink. But, on the other hand, who is there who has not known some life that was transfigured, not by the glad radiance of joy, but by its bearing the cross of pain? How many shallow people has pain deepened! How many hardening hearts has it made tender! How many has it checked, and checked effectually, when they were running headlong to their ruin! How many has it weaned from showy things, giving a vision that was fair and true, and steadying them into a sweet sobriety as if something of the unseen were in their sight! Pain may warn us of the approach of evil. It is the alarm-bell which nature rings. Pain may be used in the strong hand of God as a punishment of the sin we have committed. But never forget that far above such ministries, *pain, when it is willingly accepted, is one of the choicest instruments of purifying that is wielded by the love of heaven.* Fight against it and it shatters you. All the tools of God have double edges. Rebel against it as a thing of cruelty, and all the light of life, may be destroyed. But take it up, absorb it, in the life, weave it into the fabric of the being, and God shall bring the blossom from the thorn.

This thought, as it seems to me, may throw some light on the sufferings of the innocent.

Why Does The Innocent Suffer?

One of the hardest questions in the world is why the innocent should have to suffer so. There is no perfect answer to that question, nor ever shall be on this side of the grave. But is there not at least a partial answer in what I have been trying to say? If pain were a curse, and nothing but a curse, well might we doubt the justice on the throne; but, if pain be a ladder to a better life, then light falls on the sufferings of the innocent. It is not the anger of heaven that is smiting them. It may be the love of heaven that is blessing them. There are always tears and blood upon the steps that lead men heavenward to where the angels are. Mark you, not by the fraction of a pennyweight does that lighten the guilt of him who causes suffering. It only shows us how the love of God can take the curse and turn it to a blessing.

The Gospel and Pain

So I am led lastly to consider this, What has the Gospel done to help us to bear pain? I shall touch on three things which it has done.

1. *The Gospel has quieted those questionings which are often sorer than the pain itself.* It has helped us to believe that God is love, in the teeth of all the suffering in the world. Have you ever noticed about Jesus Christ that He was *never perplexed* by the great fact of pain? Death troubled Him, for He groaned in spirit and was troubled when He stood before the grave of Lazarus. But, though the fact of death troubled His soul, there is no trace that the dark fact of pain did so—and yet was there ever one

on earth so sensitive to pain as Jesus Christ? Here was a man who saw pain at its bitterest, yet not for an instant did He doubt His Father. Here was One who had to suffer terribly, and yet, through all His sufferings, God loved Him—it is these facts which, for the believing soul, silence the obstinate questionings forever. We may not see why we should have to suffer. We may not see why our loved ones have to suffer. Now we know in part and see in part; we are but children crying in the night. But we see Jesus, and that sufficeth us. We see how He trusted. We know how He was loved. And knowing that, we may doubt many things, but we never can doubt the love of God again, nor Christ's promise never to leave us.

2. *The Gospel has helped us here by giving us the hope of immortality.* It has set our pain in quite a new environment, that of an eternal hope. I wonder if you have ever thought of the place and power of hope in human suffering? Hope is mighty in all we have to do; but it is mighty also in all we have to bear. When once you get the glow of a great hope right in the heart of what you have to suffer, I tell you that that suffering is transfigured. Two people may have to endure an equal agony—taken abstractly, the pains are much alike,—but the one sufferer may be a hopeless man, and the other a woman with the hope of motherhood; and who shall tell the difference there is in the bearing of everything that must be borne, through the presence or the absence of such hope? It is just there that Jesus Christ steps in. He has brought immortality to light. Our light affliction, which is but for a moment, worketh for us an exceeding weight of glory. Out of Christ, we thought it was unending. We thought we never should have strength to bear it. But now, against the background of the glory, our light affliction is *but for a moment.*

3. *Christ has helped us to bear suffering by the medical science and skill he has inspired.* And I close with that, just mentioning it because I am speaking on Hospital Sunday. It has been pointed out again and again that in

the pagan world there were no hospitals. There were many noble women in that world, but not one of them ever dreamed of being a nurse. As a simple matter of historical fact, our hospitals are in the world today not because men are tenderer of heart, but because Jesus lived and Jesus died. Without Christ, we had had no Florence Nightingale—think what that would mean for British soldiers! Without Christ, we would never have had Lord Lister—think what that would have meant for countless sufferers! Without Christ, there had not been lying yonder, in the hospital which is so near me as I speak, poor men and women who are being tended by the finest skill that riches could command. For this thing will I be enquired of, saith the Lord. Yes, take a calm look at tonight. Tell me if you have ever realized what Jesus Christ has done for the community. If you have, go out and reverence Him. Go out into the night and call Him wonderful. Go out into the night and say, "God helping me, I shall follow that leader to the end."

NOTES

The Right Use of Affliction

John Calvin (1509-1564) has made his mark in history as a theologian and reformer, but he was preeminently a preacher of the Word. He ministered to the church in Geneva from 1541 to 1564, faithfully preaching the Scriptures and expounding God's truth. Weak in body, and often afflicted with pain, he nevertheless kept to a disciplined program of study and was usually at his books by five or six in the morning. That great teacher of preachers, Dr. John Broadus, said that John Calvin "gave the ablest, soundest, clearest expositions of Scripture that had been seen in a thousand years." This sermon is from *Sermons From Job,* published in 1952 by Wm. B. Eerdmans, Grand Rapids and reprinted in 1979 by Baker Book House, Grand Rapids.

13

THE RIGHT USE OF AFFLICTION

> He preserveth not the life of the wicked: but giveth judgment to the afflicted. He withdraweth not his eyes from the righteous: but with kings are they on the throne; yea, he doth establish them forever, and they are exalted. And if they be bound in fetters, and be holden in cords of affliction; then he sheweth them their work, and their transgressions that they have exceeded. He openeth also their ear to discipline, and commandeth that they return from iniquity. If they obey and serve Him, they shall spend their days in prosperity, and their years in pleasures. But if they obey not, they shall perish by the sword, and they shall die without knowledge. But the hypocrites in heart heap up wrath: they cry not when he bindeth them. They die in youth, and their life is among the unclean (Job 36:6-14).

AFTER ELIHU HAS said that, in general, God does not turn His eyes from the righteous but cares for him, and that, on the contrary, He does not enliven the wicked; he adds, particularly to better prove God's providence, that *He gives judgment to the afflicted.* For if a poor man who is utterly destitute of help and an outcast in the world is, nevertheless, delivered from affliction and persecution, the same must proceed from God. Indeed, it must be attributed to God. For if we have no support from the world, and yet have strong and powerful enemies, what is to be said except that we are lost and that there is no longer hope for our life? If, then, we are restored, it is manifest that God has been at work. So, it is not without cause that Elihu does purposely set down this saying to prove that God governs all things here below.

Also, he sets down a second example of God's providence; namely, the government by princes and by men who sit in the seat of justice, in which we perceive that God is just and that He does not will to have things to be out of order. Although there is no permanent equality, yet when we see that there is some order in the world, therein we can see as in a mirror that God has not so let loose the reigns to all confusion, that He does not still show us some sign and token of His justice. In fact, if a man considers on one side what the nature of man is, and on the other side how governors and magistrates discharge themselves; he will see and easily discern that it is a miracle of God that there is any well-being among us, and, indeed, we must know it and perceive it. I say that the nature of men is such that every man would be lord and master over his neighbors, and no man is willing to be a subject. When, then, our Lord does not permit the strong to pervail, but there is some fear and obedience toward those who are in preeminence; therein it is to be seen that God not only bridles, but also chains men's nature, in order that this pride may not raise itself so high that public government should not be above it.

Then we see that all men are given to evil and their lusts are so boiling, that every man wishes to have complete license and that no man should be under correction. Therefore, it is to be concluded, that the order of justice comes from God, and that therein He shows that He has created men in order that they should govern themselves honestly and modestly. For the second point, we see how kings and princes and those who are of lower estate behave themselves when God has armed them with the sword of justice and how they turn all things upside down, so that it seems that they wished to defy God and to destroy what He has ordained. Now, if those who ought to maintain peaceably the order constituted by God force themselves to overthrow it and deliberately fight to put things in confusion, and yet, for all that, government continues in the world, and things are not so utterly confounded that there do not still abide some marks of what God has established, is it not to be seen, thereby, that God is doubly just?

1. Therefore, it is not without cause that Elihu, after he has spoken of the relieving of the afflicted, immediately adds this example: that *God establishes kings,* and not for only a day, but in order that the same order should be continually in the world. It is true that many changes will be made from one side to the other and that there

will be great revolutions among principalities and lord-ships, but therein God shows also that it is His office to pull down the proud. Yet, even in spite of men and all their rage, some order will yet remain here below, even with respect to tyrants. If a king reigns unjustly so that he is a despiser of God and full of cruelty, violence, and insatiable covetousness; yet, notwithstanding, he must keep some shadow and appearance of justice, and he can-not go beyond it. Whence comes this, except that God thereby declares Himself? Therefore, let us learn to pro-fit in such a manner by what is seen in this world that God may be glorified in His creatures as He deserves; and above all, when we see that He delivers the poor oppressed who can do no more and who neither have, nor expect, any help from men, let us there perceive His power and His goodness, and let us be disposed to render to Him His due praise. This is what we have to observe. However, in order to prove that we are God's children, let us also be advised to lend our helping hand to those who are un-justly persecuted, according to the means which God gives us to help those who are trodden under foot and who have no means whereby to avenge or support themselves. We must consciously exert ourselves in this work.

2. Secondly, when we see that men who govern are so perverse and wicked, and yet God does not let them go entirely overboard, let us humble ourselves to honor His providence, and let us know that if He did not restrain their wickedness, we would be overwhelmed with a horri-ble flood, and everything would be immediately swal-lowed up and drowned. Therefore, God must be magnified in that we see that some residue of justice and good order remains, although those who rule and hold the sword in their hands are utterly wicked and given to all evil. So, let us know this, and let us then wholeheartedly support the order of justice, seeing that is is a sovereign benefit that God bestows upon mankind, and that therein also He wills to have His providence to be known. And when we see that princes and magistrates and all officers of justice are so perverse, let us be sorry

to see the order so profaned which God had dedicated to the salvation of men; and let us not only detest those who are enemies of God and who resist the order of government which He had set over them, but let us know that they are the fruits of our sins, in order that we may impute to ourselves the blame and the cause of all the evil. Thus, you see what we have to remember from this passage.

Now let us come to what Elihu adds. He says that if the *good men* or else the great men of whom he had spoken, whom God had exalted to high estate and dignity above the rest of the world, are sometimes *set in the stocks;* if they are sometimes brought down even in shame so that men put them in prison and in stocks and they are tied with ropes to their confounding; God does not forsake them in such necessity, but He makes them feel their sins; He tells them the faults that they have committed in order, that having known them, they may amend themselves and return to the right road; He opens their ears in order that they may think more correctly about themselves and know themselves. Elihu, then, shows here that when it seems to us that God shuts His eyes and that He no longer regards the governing of men, He has just reason to do so; and, although we find it strange, we must acknowledge that He is just and equitable in all that He does, and we have occasion to glorify Him.

It is true that what we discussed before must always be borne in mind: namely, that things are not governed in this world in a uniform manner, and that God *reserves a great part of the judgments* He intends to execute to the latter day, in order that we should always be in suspense, waiting for the coming of our Lord Jesus Christ. It ought to be sufficient for us to have some signs by which to perceive what is told us here. Now, the intention of Elihu is to anticipate the stumblingblock that men might conceive, when good and just people are trampled under foot and God exposes them to the tryanny of the wicked and they are tormented without cause, so that although they have not done wrong to anyone, yet they do not cease to be molested. For when we see this, it seems to us that

God does not think about the world, that His view does not extend to us, and that He lets fortune rule. See how our eyesight is immediately confused by our seeing things out of order, and there is nothing more easy for us than to stumble at this. For this cause, Elihu shows here that, although good men are persecuted, or else those who were advanced to power are overthrown as if God confused earth with heaven, we must not therefore be too frightened in our minds. And why? For God has just reason which we are not able to see at first glance; but let us wait in patience, and we shall know that God will make such afflictions to do us good and that they tend to a good end. And why?

"For then," he says, *"God announces to those who are so tormented by their sins,* and makes them feel what they are; it is in order to lead them to proper correction." Here we see, in the first place, that we must not estimate things according to outward appearance, but must search deeper and seek the cause that moves God to do what we find strange at first sight. It seems quite contrary to all reason that a good man should be so persecuted and that everyone should overrun him, but God knows why He does it. Therefore, we must look toward the outcome and not be too hasty to pronounce our verdict, like those who judge heedlessly.

What is the purpose of our afflictions? It is to make us feel our sins; and it is a very noteworthy point from which we can gather a mighty useful doctrine. It is true that we often hear it spoken of, yet we cannot hear it too much; for we know that afflictions are so irksome to us that every one of us frets as soon as he feels the flow of the rod at God's hand, and we cannot comfort ourselves or hold ourselves in patience. Therefore, so much the more it behooves us to note well the doctrine that when God permits us to be tormented, even unjustly, with respect to men, even then He is procuring our salvation, in that He wills to make us feel our sins and to show us what we are. For in time of prosperity we are blind; in fact we shall not know rightly what is contained here, unless God brings us to it by His chastisements.

Are we at our ease and in delights? Every one of us falls asleep, and flatters himself in his sins, so that our prosperity is like drunkenness putting our souls to sleep. And, what is worse, when God lets us alone in peace, although we have offended Him a thousand ways; yet we do not cease to applaud ourselves, and it seems to us that God is propitious toward us and that He loves us, because He does not persecute us. You see, then, that men cannot feel their sins if they are not driven by force to know themselves. Therefore, seeing that prosperity makes us so drunken after that manner, and that when we are at rest every man flatters himself in his sins, we must suffer patiently that God should afflict us. For affliction is the true school-mistress to bring men to repentance, in order that they may condemn themselves before God and, being condemned, may learn to hate their faults in which they previously bathed. Therefore, when we have known the fruit of chastisements that God sends us, we shall bear them in greater mildness and more peaceful courage than we do. But, it is pitiful how indifferent we are, because we do not know that God procures our salvation when He so afflicts us.

Besides, let us note well that we need not look at the visible hand of God to feel our faults. For it may come to pass that God will unbridle men, so that we shall be persecuted by them, even unjustly, when we shall not have done them any wrong. Yet, even in that case, we must learn that God calls us to His school. For when He refrains from striking us with His hand, but puts us into the hands of the wicked, it is to tame us and humble us better, and then He puts us to greater shame. Then, if the wicked are in control, so that they have the means to torment us, and they do to us the worst that they can; it is as if God declared to us that we are not worthy to be beaten by His own hand, and that He wills thereby to make us ashamed.

All the more ought we to be incited to think about our faults and to be sorry for them and therewithal to observe what Elihu adds, that *God then opens our ears.* This saying means two things in the Scripture. For sometimes it signifies simply to *speak to us;* and sometimes it signifies *to touch our hearts* in such a manner that we hear what is said to us. God, therefore, opens our ears when He sends us His word and causes it to be proposed to us; and then He opens our ears or He uncovers them (for the Hebrew word properly means this) when He does not permit us to be deaf to His doctrine, but He gives it entrance, in order that we may receive it and be moved by it, and that its power may be demonstrated. See the two ways of opening our ears which we daily perceive that God employs toward us.

Also, He opens the ears of those whom He afflicts in that He gives them some sign of His wrath, in order to teach them to think more correctly about themselves than they have done. If a man asks, "What then? does not God speak to us when we are in prosperity?" Yes, surely He does; but His voice cannot come to us, for we are already preoccupied with our own delights and worldly affections. In fact, we see that when men have their fill to eat, and can have a good time, and live in health and peace, they are overjoyed. Then they are so joyful that God can no longer be heard. But afflictions are messages which He sends of His wrath; then we are touched with having offended Him, in order that we may come to our senses again. So, afflictions, in general, ought to serve for instruction to those who receive them, so that they may draw near to God from Whom they had previously been estranged. So much for one point.

Yet, however, men do not let themselves be governed by God until He has softened their hearts by His Holy Spirit and opened the passage for the warnings that He gives and pierced men's ears, in order that they may dedicate themselves to His service and obedience, as it is said in the Psalm (Psalm 40:6). This is what we have to observe. Therefore, when *we are afflicted, first let us remember that it is as if God addressed Himself to us and showed us our sins and indicted us in order to draw us to repentance.* But, since we are hard to prick, and, what is more, we are utterly stubborn and deaf to all the warnings that He gives us; we must pray to Him that He may pierce our ears and make us so open to His instructions that they may be profitable to us, and that He may not merely permit the air to be beaten without touching our hearts, but that we may be moved to come and return to Him. Otherwise, let us know that we shall do nothing but provoke Him and reject His corrections, as experience shows in most men that those who are beaten with God's rods do not improve thereby, but rather grow worse. Then, since we see such examples, let us learn that nothing is done until God opens our ears; that is to say, until by His Holy Spirit He makes us listen to Him speak to us, and, having listened, also to obey Him. You see what we have to note from this passage.

He adds immediately that *if they hear and obey, they will spend their days in wealth and their years in glory, but if they do not listen to Him, they will pass by the sword and die without knowledge.* Here Elihu shows us still better the profit that we have by being in affliction. It is undoubtedly a great benefit, and one which cannot be sufficiently valued, when we are drawn to repentance and that, instead of our traveling into perdition, our Lord is bringing us back to Himself. This is what ought to sweeten all our sorrows in our afflictions. But, there is much more: namely, that our Lord shows us a proof of how profitable it is for us in order that we may be delivered from our adversities and aided by Him and that He may show that He favors us by this means.

When, then, all this is known by experience, have we not cause to be glad when God has thus delivered us? For if He let us be drunken in the pleasures of the world, in the end we would become incorrigible; therefore, He must remedy it at the right time. And if He does it by means of afflicting us and, thereupon, delivering us in order that we may perceive His hand, is it not a singular proof of His grace and of our faith? If God let us wallow in our own filthiness and in our dregs (as the Prophets term it, Jer. 48:11, Zeph. 1:12), we would rot away; and besides, we would not prize His grace toward us as it is shown to be, when He draws us out of the affliction into which we had fallen. Behold, here is a double benefit which comes back to men when God corrects them in that manner. For, in the first place, they are led back to Him; and, secondly, they perceive His fatherly goodness when they are delivered by His grace.

You see, then, what we have to observe in this passage. Now a man could ask, "Indeed, is that so? How do you know that God wills to draw us to repentance when He afflicts us or when He permits us to be tormented by men? How do we know whether or not this is His purpose or His will?" To which we answer: When we see that afflictions are temporary and God delivers us from them, let us know that He does not will to make us utterly perish, but He is contented that we are beaten down and humbled under His hand. But, when we resist Him with our brass necks and will not bow for the corrections which he sends us, we do nothing but continually double His strokes. On the contrary, then, if we feel our sins, so that we ask pardon for them and He knows that we are rightly touched by them; then He makes our afflictions to turn into a wholesome medicine for us, and, thereupon, He delivers us from them. We see all this even with our eyes.

So then, *let us not murmur any longer when we see that God sends such troubles into the world; neither let us be offended at it as if He has His eyes closed.* For He well knows what He is doing, and He has an infinite wisdom which does not appear to us at first sight; but, in the end, we surely see that He has disposed things in good order and measure.

Also, let us learn meanwhile not to be too much grieved when we are so afflicted, knowing that God does by this means further our salvation. Besides, do we wish to be healed when we are so in torment and pain? Do we wish to have a good and desirable result from them? Let us follow the way that is here shown us: namely, to hear and obey. How hear? By being taught when God holds us, as it were, in His school, so that our afflictions may be as many warnings to draw near to Him. Then, let us hear these things, and let not things go in one ear and out the other; but let us obey, that is to say, let us yield such obedience to God as we ought to do and let us not seek anything else than to frame ourselves wholly to Him. This is how we may be delivered from our adversities.

What follows? We must not be astonished if men languish in pain; indeed, if they are plunged daily deeper and deeper in their miseries. For which of them listens to God when He speaks? It is apparent that in that so many are afflicted and tormented, God's rods are busy everywhere today. But how many think about them? You will see a whole people oppressed with wars until they can stand no more; yet you will find hardly a dozen men among a hundred thousand who listen to God speak. Behold, the snapping of His whips do sound and echo in the air; there is horrible weeping and wailing everywhere; men cry, "Alas!", but meanwhile, they do not look at the hand which strikes them, as the Prophet (Isaiah 9:12) upbraids the obstinate that, though they feel the strokes, they do not acknowledge God's hand.

We see the same thing in times of pestilence and famine. So then, is it any wonder if God sends incurable wounds and does what is said by the Prophet Isaiah in 1:6, namely, that from the sole of the foot to the crown of the head there is not a drop of soundness in this people, but there is leprosy, so that they are all rotten and infected, and their sores are incurable? Is this to be wondered at, seeing that today men are so unthankful to God that they shut the door against Him and are not willing to hear Him in order to obey Him?

So then, whenever we are beaten by God's hand, *let us learn to come quickly to Him and to listen to the warnings that He gives in order that we may feel our sins and be displeased with them.* Having done that, let us be touched to the quick in order that it may please Him to have pity on us. If we proceed to it this way, God will not forget His office of instructing us and delivering us from all our adversities. But, do we wish to play we are restive horses? He will surely snub us, then, as it is said here, "We shall pass by the sword and be consumed without knowledge," that is to say, in our foolishness. When it is said, "We shall pass by the sword," the meaning is that the wounds will be utterly incurable, that we must no longer hope for healing, there will no longer be any remedy for us. If we are not obstinate when God warns us of our faults, He will show Himself a good physician toward us in purging us of them, at least if we are not incorrigible. But, if there is no reason or amendment in us so that we chew upon the bridle without feeling our sins in order to be sorry for them, let us know that all the afflictions of the world will be deadly to us.

Unless we learn to return to God when He calls us and gives us opportunity to repent, that is to say, unless we come at the right time and enter when the door is open to us; unless we do so, all the chastisements that were given us for our profit must turn to our greater condemnation and they must be so many warnings God will give, that, indeed, the heaping up of all misery upon us must be accomplished. All the more ought we to think about ourselves, that we may not knowingly provoke such vengeance of God upon us. For is it a small matter that it is said that the obstinate must be wounded by God's hand; indeed, since men as much as possible provoke Him when He has done them the favor of warning them and gives them entrance to Himself? In fact, when men chafe so, is it not open defiance of God? Is it not trampling His grace under foot? God cannot stand such spitefulness; for He swears by His majesty (Ps. 29:4, Is. 22:13), that when men make merry and say "Let us eat and drink" while God calls them to repentance, it is a sin that will never be erased. Behold, God is so irritated with that sin that He swears that it will be registered forever before Him. All the more, then, ought it to incite us to humble ourselves when God gives us some warning, knowing that He procures our salvation at this point, in order that we may not reject His yoke when He wills to put it upon us, and that we may not repulse the strokes of His rods which He gives us, as if He struck an anvil.

It is said specifically that *those who do not listen to God will die without knowledge,* that is to say, their own foolishness will consume them. This is said in order that men may be left without excuse. It is true that we surely shield ourselves with ignorance when we wish to minimize our faults or else to wipe them out completely. We say, "I did not think of it; I was not advised about it." But, let us learn that, when any mention is made of men's ignorance, it is to condemn them all the more, because they played beasts and had no reason at all in them. Even so does the Prophet Isaiah (5:13, 14) speak of it. "The very reason," says the Lord, "why hell is open and why the grave swallows up everything and why all my people are consumed is that they had no knowledge." God complains there that sinners wilfully cast themselves into destruction. However, He says that it came because they had no knowledge; indeed, but immediately He upbraids the Jews that they had become brutish. For the Lord, on His part, sufficiently warns us, so that it is our own fault if we are not well taught. How come?

God is a good schoolmaster, but we are poor scholars; God speaks, and we are deaf, or else we stop up our ears in order not to hear Him. So then the ignorance of which Elihu here speaks is voluntary, because men cannot allow God to show them their lesson or teach them to come to Him, but they would rather follow continually their ordinary path and, therefore, shut their eyes and stop up their ears. Thus, you see an ignorance that is full of malice and rebellion. Now, it is true that for a time the wicked please themselves when they do not feel God's hand, but so much the worse for them, as we see examples of it every day.

If a man speaks to these debauchers who are given to all evil and threatens them with God's vengeance, they only shake their heads and mock it and it seems to them that it is only a joke. Again, they take sermons in mockery and turn all the Holy Scripture into ridicule in order that it may no longer have reverence or authority. We see this before our eyes. They always worsen their condition, since this saying will not be frustrated: namely, that whoever is not willing to hear God in affliction must perish without knowledge; that is to say, the ignorance in which he is besotted must cause a greater ruin and plunge him deeper into God's curse.

Now, since we see this, *let us learn to be teachable, and*

*as soon as God speaks, let us give ear to Him and be ready
to subject ourselves to His word, and let nothing hinder
us from returning to Him.* This is what we are taught
in this passage. In fact, it is certain that otherwise our
own nature would always induce us to chafe against Him,
as it is said here. Besides, men's foolishness is seen in
that, although they do not wish to be considered fools and
unadvised, yet they labor to excuse themselves by folly
and ignorance when it comes to rendering their account
before God. But all this will profit them nothing. All the
more must we try to humble ourselves in good time and
to come to the comfort which God gives us when He says
that He teaches us by double means.

For, on the one side, He causes His word to be
preached to us; and, on the other side, He beats us with
His rods in order that each one of us in his own behalf
should be induced to return to the right road. Therefore,
let us have our ears open to receive the doctrine that is
set before us in the name of God, in order that He may
not speak to deaf people or tree trunks. Meanwhile, also
let us be patient in order to endure the afflictions which
He sends us; and, when something does not happen as
we would like it, let us not, therefore, ever cease to
magnify God and His grace, knowing that we may not
be so confident in them that we perish. You see, then,
that unless we wish to provoke God wilfully after we have
heard His word, we must also understand what He intends, when He chastises us and sends us some afflictions
from whatever side they may come upon us; for there shall
never happen to us anything except from His hand.

Elihu immediately adds that the hypocrites of heart lay
up wrath, and they do not cry even when they are bound;
their soul will die in youth, and they will perish with the
whoremongers. He says "hypocrites of heart." Why does
he name them so? He means those who confide in
wickedness and have a shop in the rear to hide from God
and cannot be drawn to any soundness. For we see many
poor people who sin through oversight, because they are
fickle so that they are easily debauched, and yet there
is no malicious or rooted obstinacy in them. But, there

are others who are "hypocrites of heart," that is to say, who have in them the root of contempt and of all rebellion, so that they mock God and have no reverence for His word; but the devil has so bewitched them that they condemn the good and follow the evil or at least approve it, and they wish to delight in it and to feed upon it.

Therefore, let us note well that when Elihu speaks here of "hypocrites of heart" he means those who are so wholly abandoned to Satan that they sin not only through oversight but are wholly framed to evil that they are fully bent on doing evil and mocking God; and of such men too many examples are seen. For if a man includes those who are fickle and who offend through weakness with the wicked and the despisers of God, the number of the wicked will be far greater. Let us note that it is not without cause that Elihu calls them hypocrites of heart, or perverse of heart, that is to say, utterly given to extreme maliciousness, so that in their afflictions they are not willing in any manner to subject themselves to God, but rather heap up wrath.

Let us note well the phrase "heaping up wrath"; for it is like kindling the fire still more and more, and throwing on wood to augment it. In fact, what are the perverse doing when they strive and fret so against God? Do they improve their case or condition? Alas! They only heap up more wood, and the wrath of God must burn hotter. So then, let us remember well that if we resist God's chastisements, thinking to repulse them by our malice and obstinacy, we shall only increase wrath, and God's curse will be augmented more and more until we are utterly consumed by it. Now, when we hear this, what have we to do except to pray to God that, in the first place, He may so purge us that we may not have this rebellion rooted in us and this malice hidden; but, although we have filed through infirmity, yet there may always be some root of the fear of God in us, so that we may not become utterly incorrigible. Also, let us be advised always to conduct ourselves in sobriety and singleness of heart in order that we may not be so wrapped in our sins that we like them and feed upon them. Morever, let us note well that if we wish to work wiles and tricks upon God, it will not improve our status, but rather we shall increase His wrath against us.

You see, then, that men ought to correct properly their evil doings, seeing that God's curse will be so increased upon them. And here is express mention made of the increasing of God's wrath, because men suppose they have escaped when God has delivered them from some ill; it seems to them that the worst is past. But, we do not think about the means which are hidden from us: namely, that God will afterwards display new rods, that He will draw new swords, and that He will suddenly thunder upon us when we do not expect it. Since, then, we are not sufficiently afraid of God's wrath, therefore, it is purposely said that it increases and that we heap it up more and more upon us, insomuch that a hundred thousand deaths must be waiting for us when we have despised the message which God sent to bring us back and to lead us into life. Therefore, when we have so despised God's warnings, we must feel His horrible vengeance upon us, whereas, otherwise He affirms that He is always ready to comfort those who submit themselves willingly to His good will.

The Sea of Glass Mingled With Fire

Phillips Brooks (1835-1893) was ordained
into the Protestant Episcopal Church in 1860
while serving in Philadelphia. He became
minister of Trinity Church, Boston, in 1869,
and served there for twenty-two years. In 1891
he was ordained Bishop of Massachusetts. He
is best known for his *Lectures on Preaching*
which he delivered at Yale in 1877. He
published many volumes of sermons and lectures. This sermon is taken from *Twenty Sermons*, by Phillips Brooks, and published in
1886 by MacMillan and Co., London.

Phillips Brooks

14

THE SEA OF GLASS MINGLED WITH FIRE

And I saw as it were a sea of glass mingled with fire; and them that had gotten the victory over the beast . . . stand on the sea of glass, having the harps of God (Revelation 15:2).

WITH ALL THE mysteriousness of the Book of Revelation, one thing we are sure of: in it we have the summing up of the moral processes of all time. There may or may not be a more special meaning discoverable in its pictures, but this there certainly is. Many people find great pleasure in tracing out elaborate analogies between its prophecies and certain particular events in the world's history. "Here," they cry, pointing to some particular event of contemporary history, "do you not see that this is what these chapters mean?" "Yes," we may generally answer, "they very possibly do mean that, but they mean so much besides that. They mean that, and all other events in which the same universal and eternal causes were at work. These special examples fall in under them, but do not certainly exhaust their application. They are much larger and include much more. They take in the whole circle of great spiritual and moral principles."

In this way I look at, and shall ask you to study with me, the verse which is our text. I take it to represent, in a highly figurative way, the result of all moral contest. We may call that our subject.

It surely is no unimportant one. It is a subject that ought to touch all of us very closely, to waken our interest and deep anxiety. I am not to speak to you of imaginary or unreal conditions, not of unheard of depths of sin, or unimagined heights of holy rapture, but only of moral contest, of this struggle with suffering and wickedness, of trial, of that state which every earnest man who is conscious of his own inner life at all knows full well. What is to be the end of it all? How is it all coming out? These are the questions for which I find some suggestion of an answer in the pictorial prophecy of John.

They who had gotten the victory over the Beast stood on a sea of glass, mingled with fire. What is the meaning of this imagery? I confess that I do not pretend to know in full what is intended in the Revelation by this term "the Beast." But on the principle which I just stated, I think it certainly means in its largest sense the whole power of evil in all its earthly manifestations; everything that tempts the soul of man to sin or tries his patience with suffering. Others assert more personal meanings for the name. One very large school says that it means the Church of Rome; another set of commentators used to make "the Beast" to be Napoleon the Third. Perhaps the name may well include them both, in so far as both stand for badness and mischief in the world; but for our present purpose at least, it will be well not to meddle with any of that sort of partial, precarious interpretation, but to hold what certainly is true, that "the Beast," in its largest sense, means all that is beastly, all that is low and base and tries to drag down what is high and noble, all sin and temptation; and so that "they who have gotten the victory over the Beast," are they who have come out of sin holy, and out of trial pure, and out of much tribulation have entered into the kingdom of heaven.

These are to walk upon "a sea of glass, mingled with fire." What does that imagery mean? The sea of glass, the glassy sea, with its smooth transparency settled into solid stillness without a ripple or the possibility of a storm, calm, clear, placid—evidently that is the type of repose, of rest, of peace. And fire, with its quick, eager, searching nature, testing all things, consuming what is evil, purifying what is good, never resting a moment, never sparing pain; fire, all through the Bible, is the type of active trial of every sort, of struggle. "The fire shall try every man's work of what sort it is." "The sea of glass," then, "mingled with fire," is repose mingled with struggle. It is peace and rest and achievement, with the power of trial and suffering yet alive and working within it. It is calmness still pervaded by the discipline through which it has been reached.

This is our doctrine—the permanent value of trial—that when a man conquers his adversaries and his difficulties, it is not as if he never had encountered them. Their power, still kept, is in all his future life. They are not only events in his past history, they are elements in all his present character. His victory is colored with the hard struggle that won it. His sea of glass is always mingled with fire, just as this peaceful crust of earth on which we live, with its wheat fields, vineyards, orchards and flower-beds, is full still of the power of the convulsion that wrought it into its present shape, of the floods and volcanoes and glaciers which have rent it, or drowned it, or tortured it. Just as the whole fruitful earth, deep in its heart, is still mingled with the ever-burning fire that is working out is chemical fitness for its work, just so the life that has been overturned and overturned by the strong hand of God, filled with the deep revolutionary forces of suffering, and purified by the strong fires of temptation, keeps its long discipline forever, and roots in that discipline the deepest growths of the most sunny and luxuriant spiritual life that it is ever able to attain.

How wide this doctrine is. The health of the grown man is something different from the health of the little child, because it has been reached through so many strains and tests and dangers. His strong body carries within it not only the record, but the power, of all that it has passed through. His bones are strong by every tug and wrench and burden they have borne. His pulse beats even and true with the steady purposeful power which it has learned from many a period of feverish excitement. His blood flows cool, his eye is clear with the simple and healthy action which they have gathered out of many a time of danger that has come since the rosy untried health of babyhood. He is stronger by the accumulated strength of trial. His sea of glass in mingled with fire.

So take the strong man who has won a large property through many disappointments and reverses, and compare him with the baby of fortune who has just inherited money which he never earned. Compare the rich fathers who have made the fortunes with the rich sons who spend them. Is there no keener and more intelligent sense of the value of money in one than in the other? Sometimes indeed the sense is only keener and not more intelligent. Sometimes the father is a miser, while the son is a pattern of judicious liberty. These differences are personal; but always, either for good or bad, the old contest, the long, hard days of patience, the courage, the perseverance which earned the fortune color its whole possession and use. The repose of old age is full of the character that came from the early struggle. The sea of glass is mingled with fire.

Or, shall we take the man whose life has known bereavement, who has passed sometime through those days and nights which I may not try to describe to you, but which come up to so many of you as I say the old word, death? Days and nights when he watched the slow untwisting of some silver cord on which his very life was hung, or suddenly felt the golden bowl, dash down and broken, of which his very life had drunk. The first shock became dulled. The first agony grew calm. The lips subsided into serenity. But was there not something in him that made him greater and purer and richer than of old; something that let any one see who watched the change, that it was "better to have loved and lost than never to have loved at all." A whole new quality, that rich quality which the Bible calls by its large word "patience," the power of his trial, was in his new serenity, until he died. His sea of glass was always mingled with fire.

So it is with the world; so it is with nations. A people that has fought for its life, that has had its institutions and ideas subjected to the fiery ordeal, can never be again what it has been. It is not simply older by so many years, but deeper and truer by so much suffering. Besides the mere value which men learn to put into what they have had to fight for, however worthless it may be in itself, the nation that has been saved by struggle, if it has faith enough to believe that it was really saved by struggle and not by accident, by the strength of its ideas and not by the chance of turning of the weather-cock of battle, must always, in whatever times of peace may follow, deal with its ideas with greater reverence for the strength that has come out of them in war. Under its safest security it will always want to feel still the capacity for the same vigorous self-defense if it should ever again be needed. Thus its sea of glass will always be mingled with fire.

These are illustrations of our doctrine. But the trouble will be that, however much we recognize the general rule, the exceptions to it, the variations in the effect of trial upon character, will be so numerous as to perplex us. We meet with so many people whose character seems not to be elevated or fired, but depressed and smothered, by suffering. They come out of adversity apparently with a great loss of what was noblest and most attractive in them before. Men who were smooth and gracious in health, become rough and peevish in sickness. Men who were cordial and liberal in wealth, turn proud and reserved and tight as poverty overtakes them. If trial kindles and stirs up some sluggish natures, on the other hand it quenches and subdues many vigorous and ardent hearts and sends them crushed and self-distrustful to their graves. It seems sometimes as if trouble, trial and suffering were in the world like the old fabulous river in Epirus of which the legend ran—that its wonderful waters kindled every unlighted torch that was dipped into them, and quenched every torch that was lighted.

But, however much difficulty this may give us in single cases, it fits in well with our general doctrine. *For it makes trial an absolutely necessary element in all perfected character.* If so much character does really go to pieces at its first contact with suffering and struggle, then all the more, no matter how terrible the waste may be, we see the need of keeping struggle and suffering as tests of character. We see that to sweep them away would be both an insult and a cruel harm to the nature which was meant to meet them, to crush and conquer and analyze them, to assimilate their strength out of them as a plant assimilates the nutriment out of the hindering ground through which it has to fight its way up into the sunshine, and to grow strong by struggle. You may just fling your seed upon the surface, and it will easily come to a sort of sickly germination. It has no earth to fight its way through, but then it has no earth to feed upon either; and the first of it is almost the last of it too.

We cannot exaggerate the importance of the change which comes to pass in a man's life when he once thoroughly has learned this simple truth. Disappointments of every sort, sorrows, suffering, trials, struggles, restlessness and dissatisfaction, false friends, poor health, low tastes and standards all about us—who shall enumerate the million forms, new to each man's new appreciation, in which life is to each man dark and not bright, bitter and not sweet? Who shall catalog the troubles of human life? But who shall tell the difference between two men who live in different aspects of all these things? Are they intrusions, accidents, thwartings and disappointments of the will of God? Or, are they (this is what our doctrine says they are) Messiahs, things sent, having like the ships that sail to our ports from far-off lands of barbarian richness, rare spices and fragrant oils and choice foods that we cannot find at home, whose foreign luxuriance forces its odorous way through the coarse and uncouth coverings in which their wealth was packed away in the savage lands from which they came? Are the prolific sources of spiritual culture, contributing what our best happiness could not have except from them, the energy and vitality which there is no way of stirring up in human nature but by some sense of danger, the fire to mingle with the glass.

In sick-rooms, in prisons, in dreary, unsympathetic homes, in stores where failure brooded like the first haze of coming eastern storms, everywhere where men have suffered, to some among the sufferers this truth has come. They lifted up their heads and were strong. Life was a new thing to them. They were no longer the victims of a mistaking chance or of a malignant devil, but the subjects of an educating God. They no longer just waited doggedly for the trouble to pass away. They did not know that it would ever pass away. If it ever did, it must go despoiled of its power. Whether it passed or stayed, that was not the point, but that the strength that was in it should pass into the sufferer who wrestled with it; that the fire should not only make the glass and then go out, leaving it cold and hard and brittle. The fire must abide in the glass that it has made, giving it forever its own warmth and life and elastic toughness. This is the great revelation of the permanent value of suffering.

But some lives still grow old, some men live strongly and purely in this world, you say, and then go safely and serenely to heaven, who have no struggle anywhere, who never know what struggle is. What shall we say of them? How are they ripened and saved? How does the fire get into their sea of glass? Ah, my dear friend, first you must find your man. You may search all the ages for him. You may go through the crowded streets of heaven, asking each saint how he came there, and you will look in vain everywhere for a man morally and spiritually strong, whose strength did not come to him in struggle. Will you take the man who never had a disappointment, who never knew a want, whose friends all love him, whose health never knew a suspicion of its perfectness, on whom every sun shines and against whose sails all winds, as if by special commission, are sent to blow, and who still is great and good and true and unselfish and holy, as happy in his inner as in his outer life? Was there no struggle there? Do you suppose that man has never prayed, and emphasized his prayer with labor, "In all time of my prosperity, Good Lord, deliver me!" "Deliver me!"—That is the cry of a man in danger, of a man with an antagonist. For years that man and his prosperity have been looking each other in the face and grappling one another. Whether he should rule it or it should rule him, that was the question. He saw plenty of men whose prosperity ruled them, had them for its slaves, and bound them, drove them, beat them, taunted them, and mocked them with the splendid livery it made them wear, which was only the symbol of their servitude to it: that dreadful prosperity of theirs which they must obey, no matter what it asked of them, to which they must give up soul and body. He was determined it should not be so with him. He wrestled with his prosperity and mastered it. His soul is not the slave of his rich store or of his comfortable house. They are the slaves of his soul. They must minister to its support and culture. *He* rules *His,* and that is a supremacy that was not won without a struggle, than which there is no harder on earth.

So that even here there is no exception. There is no exception anywhere. Every true strength is gained in struggle. Every poor soul that the Lord heals and frees goes up the street like the man at Capernaum, carrying its bed upon its back, the trophy of its conquered palsy. These are no glassy seas which will really bear the weight of strong men but those that have the fiery mingling. All others are counterfeits, and these crack or break.

There are several special applications of our doctrine to the Christian life, which it is interesting to observe.

1. It touches all the variations of Christian feeling. In almost every Christian's experience come times of despondency and gloom, when there seems to be a depletion of the spiritual life, when the fountains that used to burst and sing with water are grown dry; when love is loveless, hope hopeless, and enthusiasm so utterly dead and buried, that it is hard for us to believe that it ever lived. At such times, there is nothing for us to do but hold with eager hands to the bare, rocky truths of our religion as a shipwrecked man hangs to a strong, ragged cliff when the great retiring wave and all the little eddies all together are trying to sweep him back into the deep. The rough rock tears his hands, but he still clings to it. And so the bold, bare truths of God and Christ, of responsibility and eternity are stripped for the time of all the dearness that they used to have. How sometimes we have just to clutch and hold fast by them in our darkness to keep from being swept off into recklessness and despair. Then when the tide returns, and we can hold ourselves lightly where we once had to hang heavily, when faith grows easy and God and Christ and responsibility and eternity are once

more the glory and delight of happy days and peaceful nights, then certainly there is something new in them, a new color, a new warmth. The soul has caught a new idea of God's love when it has not only been fed but rescued by Him. The sheep has a new conception of his shepherd's care when he has not merely been made "to lie down in green pastures," but also has heard the voice of him who had left the ninety and nine in the wilderness and gone after that which had wandered astray, until he found it. The weakness of our own nature and the strength of that on which we rely: danger and its correlative, duty; watchfulness, and its great privilege, trust, come in together, and are the new life of the soul, the active power in its restored peace, the fire in its glassy sea.

The same applies to doubt and belief. "Why do things seem so hard to me?" you say. "Why does every conceivable objection and difficulty start up in a moment, just as soon as I attempt to lay hold upon the Christian's faith? Why is it so easy for these others to believe, so hard for me?" One cannot answer certainly until he knows you better. There is a willful and an unwilling unbelief. If it is willful unbelief, the fault is yours. Man must not certainly complain that the sun does not shine on him, because he shuts his eyes. But if it is unwilling unbelief; if you really want the truth; if you are not afraid to submit to it as soon as you shall see it, and it is something in your constitution, or in your circumstances, or in the side of Christian truth that has been held out to you that makes it more difficult for you to grasp it than your neighbor; then you are not to be pitied. You have a higher chance than he. To climb the mountain on its hardest side, where its rough granite ribs press out most ruggedly to make your climbing difficult, where you must skirt round chasms and clamber down and up ravines, all this has its compensations. You know the mountain better when you reach its top. It's a nobler and so a dearer thing.

2. If there be such here, let me speak to them. The world has slowly learned that Christianity is true. If you learn slowly, it is only the old way over again. The man who

who learns slowly, learns completely, if he learns at last at all. If you can only keep on bravely, perseveringly, seeking the truth, saying I must have it or I die; saying that until you do die; dying at last, if need be, in the search; then I declare not only that somewhere, here or in some better world, the truth shall come to you; but that when it comes, the peace and the serenity of it shall be made vital with the energy of your long search. Yours shall be that faith with which a pure, truth-loving soul may stand unashamed before the throne of God, and hear his work called "Well-done," and blessed and consecrated to perpetual value. You will believe better even in heaven for these earthly difficulties bravely met. For perfect truthfulness must find the truth at last, or where is God?

3. As we look out, the applications of our doctrine widen everywhere. What is the whole history of the world under the Gospel of forgiveness, from its first to its last, but one vast application of it. Here are men whose condition as perverted, mistaken, sinful beings makes it absolutely necessary that the dispensation that shall save them must be one, not of mere culture and development, of rescue and repentance. Let the great future of those men be what it will; let the sublimest regions of calm, unbroken holiness be reached in some celestial sphere, let truth and godliness become the atmosphere and the unconscious life-blood of the perfected man, still the perfected man must carry, somewhere in the nature which holds high converse with the angels and worships with affectionate awe close to the throne of God, the story of its sin and its escape. Redeemed, its great redemption must forever be the shaping element of all its glorious life. "Worthy is He who hath redeemed us"—that song the purest lips and the most exalted heart never will outgrow.

Simon Peter is forgiven, re-adopted, becomes the preacher of the first sermon, the converter of the first Gentiles, the founder of churches, the writer of epistles, the champion of faith; but he is always, to the last, the same Simon Peter who denied his Master and struggled with himself in all the bitterness of tears, upon the crucifixion

night. Paul mounts up to the third heaven, hears wonderful voices, sees unutterable things, can give in bold humility
the autobiography of the eleventh chapter to the Corinthians, but he never ceases to be the Paul who stood by
at the stoning of Stephen, and had his great darkness rent
assunder by the bright light that he saw upon the road from
Jerusalem to Damascus. You and I, brethren, come by
Christ's grace into sweet communion with God, but the
power of our conversion—does it ever leave us?

Are not we prodigals still, with the best robe and the ring
and the shoes upon us, and the fatted calf before us in our
father's house, conscious always that our filial love is full
of the strength of hard repentance which first made us turn
our faces homeward from among the swine? And so the saved world never can forget that it was once the lost world.
All of a history such as it has been accumulates, and none
of it is lost. It will forever shine with a peculiar light, sing
a psalm among its fellows that shall be all its own. The
redeemed world—all the strong vitality which that name
records, will be the fire that will mingle with the glassy
serenity of its obedient and rescued life.

4. Here, then, we have the picture of the everlasting
life. What will heaven be? What will be the substance
on which they shall stand who worship God and praise
him in the ages of eternity? I find manifold fitness in the
answer that tells us that it shall be a "sea of glass mingled
with fire." Is it not a most graphic picture of that experience of rest always pervaded with activity; of calm,
transparent contemplation, always pervaded and kept
alive by eager work and service, which is our highest and
most Christian hope of heaven? Let us be sure that our
expectations regarding heaven are scriptural and true.
Heaven will not be pure stagnation, not idleness, not any
mere luxurious dreaming over the spiritual repose that
has been safely and forever won; but active, tireless,
earnest work; fresh, lively enthusiasm for the high labors
which eternity will offer. These vivid inspirations will
play through our deep repose and make it more mighty
in the service of God than any feverish and unsatisfied

toil of earth has ever been. The sea of glass will be mingled with fire.

5. Here, too, we have the type and standard of that heavenliness of character which ought to be ripening in all of us now, as we are getting ready for that spiritual life. As men by the grace of God gradually win the "victory over the beast," they begin already to walk upon the sea of glass mingled with fire. Let this be the lesson with which we close our thought upon our text. Surely, dear friends, there is a very high and happy life conceivable, which very few of us attain, and yet which our religion most evidently intends for all of us. Calm and yet active; peaceful and yet thoroughly alive; resting always completely upon truth, but never sleeping on it for a moment; working always intensely, but serene and certain of results, never driven crazy by our work; grounded and settled, yet always moving forward in still, but sure, progress; always secure and alert—glass mingled with fire.

That life, which we dream of in ourselves, we see in Jesus. Where was there ever gentleness so full of energy? What life as still as his was ever so pervaded with untiring and restless power? Who ever knew the purposes for which he worked to be so sure, and yet so labored for them as if they were uncertain? Who ever believed his truths so entirely, and yet believed them so vividly as Jesus? Such perfect peace that never grew listless for a moment; such perfect activity that never grew restless or excited; these are the wonders of the life of Him who going up and down the rugged ways of Palestine, was spiritually walking on "the sea of glass mingled with fire."

As more and more we get the victory over the beast, we, too, are lifted up to walk where he walked. For this, all trial, all suffering, and all struggle are sent. May God grant us all much of that grace through which we can be "more than conquerers through him who loved us," and so begin now to "walk with him in white" upon "the sea of glass mingled with fire."

NOTES

Tears of Jesus

Frederick W. Robertson (1816-1853)
wanted to be a soldier, but he yielded to his
father's decision that he take orders in the
Anglican church. The courage that he would
have shown on the battlefield, he displayed in
the pulpit, where he fearlessly declared truth
as he saw it. Never strong physically, he ex-
perienced deep depression, he questioned his
faith, and he often wondered if his ministry
was doing any good. He died a young man, in
great pain, but in great faith and courage. He
had ministered for only six years at Trinity
Chapel, Brighton, but today his printed sermons have taken his brave message around
the world. This one is from his *Sermons, Fifth
Series,* published in 1900 in London by Kegan
Paul, Trench, Trubner and Company. It is but
a "skeleton" summary, yet it contains more
truth than some complete sermons by others!

F.W. Robertson

15

TEARS OF JESUS

Jesus wept (John 11:35).

CHRISTIANITY is God manifest in the flesh.

Christianity is contained in the life of Jesus Christ. To adore Christ, love Christ, trust Christ: that is Christianity.

Not dogmas about Christ, but Christ. This is the Gospel. The spirit of the life with which Christ lived—His character. Therefore, we must understand Christ, and this as a whole made up of many particulars.

Imagine a spectator advancing towards the earth—pausing at 10,000 miles distance—contemplating a glorious star—then alighting on a mountain—then arriving below, and finding it peopled; a history to every spot, a science in every stone, in every atom the study of life. To understand this earth, which looked to be one bright mass, is to be in possession of every science and every history: to know it in its atoms and to know it as a whole.

So with Christ. We by degrees master that character, till we find it boundless. Thought and depth in every sentence. Few men know much of Christ—none the whole! Christianity dwells entire only in one bosom.

Some comprehend His reformation of abuses; others His abhorrence of pretense in religion; others His assertion of man's equality; others His purity, His courage, His truth; others the merely human aspect of His character, but His character is a whole!

There are persons who write treatises on one country's history—others on the structure of a plant. Only a few, like Herschel and Humboldt, can comprehend with something like adequateness the cosmos or order of the universe. There is no one who cannot read a page of it:—but "to be able to compose Cosmos!"* (*Influence of Poetry*).

Bear this in mind. We contemplate now one feeling only: "Jesus wept."

Our subject divides itself into two branches:
1. Causes of Christ's sorrow and
2. Its peculiar character.

Causes of Christ's Sorrow

1. *The possession of a soul.*
When we speak of Deity joined to humanity, we do not mean joined to a body. Not a body inhabited by Deity, as our bodies are by soul. But, we mean Deity joined to manhood—body *and* soul. With a body only, Jesus might have wept for hunger, but not wept for sorrow. That is neither the property of Deity nor of body, but of soul.

Humanity in Christ was perfect. The possession of a body enabled Him to weary; the possession of a soul capacitated Him to weep.

2. *The spectacle of human sorrow.* And this twofold: Death of a friend: "Behold how he loved him."

Sorrow of two friends: "When Jesus therefore saw her weeping. . . . Jesus wept."

The death of His friend was a cause of the sorrow of Jesus.

Mysterious! Jesus knew that He could raise him. All-knowing wisdom; all-powerful strength. Yet, "Jesus wept."

This is partly intelligible. Conceptions strongly presented produce effects like reality, *e.g.* we wake dreaming, our eyes suffused with tears, we know it is a dream, yet tears flow on.

To say that Jesus wept is only to say that His humanity was perfect; that His mind moved by the same laws as ours.

Moreover, it was only delay. One day Lazarus would die, and the mourning would be real.

Now, observe, the sadness of Jesus for His friend is what is repeated with us all. The news comes—"He whom thou lovest is sick," and then in two days more news—"Lazarus is dead." Startling! Somehow we twine our hearts around men we love as if forever. Death and anyone we love are not thought of in connection with each other. He die! He die? Fartherest thought from our mind. Shocking thought.

It is a shock to find the reality of this awful life: that we are swimming on a sea of appearances—floating on an eternity that gives way. These attachments, loves, etc., they do not hold; there is no firmness in them. We are, and then, suddenly, we are not. Life and death, what are they?

Next, the sorrow of His two friends caused the tears of Jesus.

Look at this family. Three persons: a brother lost, two surviving sisters.

The sisters' characters were diverse. Martha found her life in the outer world of fact; Mary in the inner world of feeling. They are types of the practical and the contemplative.

Their way of manifesting feeling is different. Martha expressed herself outwardly in word, in action, in small acts of attention; she loved to discuss earnestly with the intellect the question of resurrection—contended how things might have been otherwise. Mary did not express; felt herself inexpressible; reached truth by the heart, not by the mind—lived in contemplation. In manhood, one would have found life in the storm of the world; the other in retirement. As students, one would have studied the outward life of man in history; the other, philosophy, the causes of things, the world visible, and the stranger world within.

Two links bound these diverse characters together: love for Lazarus and attachment to the Redeemer. And this true union—similars in dissimilarity, worlds differing, spheres differing, yet no clashing—bound them together by one common pursuit.

Now, one link was gone. Of him, Lazarus, we know little. Only he was one whom Jesus loved, and he had the strong attachment of such women as Martha and Mary.

His loss was not an isolated fact. The family was broken up, the sun of the system was gone, and the planets were no longer revolving round a center harmoniously. The keystone is removed from the arch and the stones are losing their cohesion. There were points of repulsion, too, manifest even in life. They could not understand one another's different modes of feeling: Martha complains of Mary at the feast. Lazarus gave them a common tie. That removed, the points of repulsion would daily become more sharp and salient.

Over the breaking up of a family, Jesus wept.

And this is what makes death sad. Let him who calls death a trifle remember this—not that one man is gone, but that Bethany is no longer Bethany. A blight is there. You open a book, there is a name. A day comes, it is a birthday—the chair is vacant. In reverie, you half rise up, but the name on your lips belongs to none on earth.

Character of Christ's Sorrow

What was the spirit in which Jesus saw this death?

1. *Calmly:* "Lazarus sleepeth." It is the world of repose where all is placid.

Struggling men have tried to forget this restless world, and slumber like a babe—tired, yea, tired at heart. Lazarus is stretched-out to his Divine friend's imagination, but he lies calm. The long day's work is done—the hands are folded. Nothing to fret now but the "small cold" worm. Waves of shadow are flying over the long grass on his grave.

Friends are gathered to praise, enemies to slander. But praise and slander on his ear make no impression. Conscious he is perhaps elsewhere; but unconscious of earthly noise. Musketry over grave—requiem mass—minstrels making a noise. . . . All this is for the living—the dead hear not. But, "he sleeps well." That is the tone of feeling with which to stand over the Christian's deathbed: "Our friend Lazarus sleepeth."

2. *Sadly.* Hence, observe Jesus permitted sorrow.

Great Nature is wiser than we. We recommend weeping, or prate about submission, or say all must die. Nature, God, say, "Let nature rule, to weep or not."

Do you say tears imply selfishness or distrust? I answer: Weep. Let grief be law to herself. We infer that grief is no distrust of God—no selfishness. Sorrow is but love without its object.

3. *Hopefully.* "I go that I may awake him out of sleep: thy brother shall rise again" (John 11:11, 23). Not merely calmness, nor sadness, nor sorrow, nor despair, but hope.

Observe, the amount of hope depends on character and imaginative power.

Sanguine minds are elastic; it is very easy for them to blame deeper shadow, as if that which is natural-spirits were all faith.

Allowance, too, must be made for imaginative power. That is the world of shadows; this the world of experience and recollection. Some persons live in the past more than in the future. Others there are who travel with the sun ever before them, keeping pace with the sun.

Hope will be small when imagination is scanty; but feebleness of hope is not feebleness of faith.

4. *In reserve*—the reserve of sorrow.

On the first announcement, Jesus speaks not a word. When He met the mourners He offered them no commonplace consolation. He is less anxious to exhibit feeling than to soothe. But Nature had her way at last. Yet even then, by act more than by word, the Jews inferred He loved him: "Jesus wept. *Then* said the Jews, Behold how he loved him!" (John 11:35, 36).

There is the reserve of nature and the reserve of grace.

We have our own English reserve: we do not give way to feeling. We respect grief when it does not make an exhibition. An Englishman is ashamed of his good feelings as much as of his bad ones. In sarcasm, sneer, and hummed tune, tears will be concealed. All this is neither good nor bad—it is nature.

But let it be sanctified; let reserve of nature pass into reserve of Christian delicacy.

Let us add a few words of application.

In this there is consolation for us. But consolation is not the privilege of all sorrow. Christ is at Lazarus' grave, because Christ had been at the sisters' home; sanctifying their joys, and their very meals. They had anchored on the rock in sunshine, and in the storm the ship held to her moorings.

The heart is desolate which seeks a Savior first when cut away by force. He who has lived with Christ will find Christ near in death. "I will never leave you" (Hebrews 13:5).

If you choose duty—God—it is not so difficult to die.

NOTES

When Worn With Sickness

William E. Sangster (1900-1960) was the "John Wesley" of his generation as he devoted his life to evangelism and the promoting of practical sanctification. He pastored in England and Wales, and his preaching ability attracted the attention of the Methodist leaders. He ministered during World War II at Westminster Central Hall, London, where he pastored the church, managed an air-raid shelter in the basement, and studied for his Ph.D. at the London University! He served as president of the Methodist Conference (1950) and director of the denomination's home missions and evangelism ministry. He published several books on preaching, sanctification, and evangelism, as well as volumes of sermons. This message comes from *He is Able,* published in 1936 by Hodder and Stoughton, London.

William E. Sangster

16

WHEN WORN WITH SICKNESS

STUDDERT KENNEDY used to say that a man who was un-disturbed by the problem of pain was suffering from one of two things: either from a hardening of the heart, or a softening of the brain. And Kennedy was right! Everyone who is mentally alive, especially if he believes in a God of love, finds this problem difficult of solution; because it must be admitted, even by the keenest believer in spiritual healing, that some sicknesses are proof against every effort at cure. Neither the prayer of faith, nor the skill of the doctor, avail. The disease takes its dread, unhindered course, and love's only ministry is to palliate the pain. Even this is not always possible. One must sometimes stand by and see a dear one racked out of human shape and yet be incapable of any useful ser-vice. Death is not the deepest mystery. We must all die, but pain...!

Sir Arthur Conan Doyle tells in his autobiography, what it was that made him a materialist in early life. As a physician, he constantly saw sights which he could not reconcile with the idea of a merciful providence.

> I was called in by a poor woman to see her daughter. As I entered the humble sitting-room, there was a small cot on one side, and by the gesture of the mother I understood that the sufferer was there. I picked up a candle and, walking over, I stooped over the little bed expecting to see a child. What I really saw was a pair of brown sullen eyes, full of loathing and pain, which looked up in resentment to mine. I could not tell how old the creature was. Long thin limbs were twisted and coiled in the tiny couch. The face was sane, but malignant. "What is it?," I asked in dismay, when we were out of hearing, "It's a girl," sobbed the mother. "She's nineteen. Oh! If God would only take her!" (*Memories and Adventures*, p. 83.)

There are some people so shallow of mind or unfeeling of heart, that they can chatter cheerfully even in the presence of a problem like that. Sometimes they prattle about a deficiency of faith in the sufferer, and some suggest that God would cure the whole thing tomorrow, if only the subject would "believe". Is it possible that they do not know that some of the world's profoundest saints have had to walk this way? Sometimes they suggest that pain is an unsubstantial bogey of our minds, a mere figment of a diseased imagination, having no basis in reality and curable by some simple re-adjustment of our thought. Is it possible that they can look on an acute case of rheumatoid arthritis, a body twisted to inhuman shapes, or stand, in the last stages, by a cancerous death-bed and really believe themselves that this is some figment of a diseased imagination? The world does not doubt that it is a healthy thing to fill the mind with strong positive thoughts, to the exclusion of self-pity and hypochondria, but when that modicum of widely-received truth is carried over and asserted as a cure of pain and sickness as a whole, the mind rebels against such impositions. Not by the cultivation of superior forms of self-deception can this problem be solved. It must be faced in all its naked hideousness. Is Christ able to succor us when we are worn with sickness; when every known resource of healing— spiritual, mental, and medical—has failed? Can He keep us brave, if not blithe; at peace, if not in joy? Is He able?

The Need to Trust God

We *know* that He is able. We believe that in the same way as human parents must sometimes allow pain and discipline to press upon their dearly-loved children, so must the gracious Father in Heaven allow pain and discipline to press upon us, not in any neglectful and unloving spirit, but for some high and holy purpose known to Him. Though He does not will the calamities, He wills the conditions in which these calamities are possible. We believe also that, when we cannot interpret the dark mystery of life, and God seems indifferent to our plea for explanations, it is not because there is no meaning in it, or because He does not know, or does not care. It is just because, as yet, our minds are too small and we cannot take the explanation in. We have reached that stage in human development when we are able to ask the questions, but are not always able to understand the answers. God expects us to trust His love.

I remember that when my son had a nasal growth removed, he was between three and four years of age. The little operation was being performed on a number of other children at the same time, and the surgeon's waiting room was crowded. Unhappily, the slight accommodation made it necessary for each little patient, as the operation was completed, to cross the corner of the room where the others were waiting to go in, and complete concealment was not possible. They heard the cries, saw the blood, and a tempest of questions rose to my son's lips. He said: "Must I go in there? Will the nurse be coming for me? Will it hurt? What is it all for?"

Well, what can you say to a child of three and a half? You cannot talk about tonsilitis, or lymphoid tissue, or septic infection. You must just fall back upon generalities. You say: "I must not save you from it, dear. You will understand someday. You must trust my love." And when the moment comes, you put him firmly in the nurse's arms for an experience which you know will be painful and nauseating, but which, for the child's sake, you are determined to see through.

That seems to be a fair parallel of how God deals with us. In the vast affairs of this universe, we are old enough to ask questions, but our minds are not yet big enough to understand all the answers. God says, "Trust my love." Can we not trust Him though He leads us in the path which is so darkly wise?

The time of suffering is not a time for speech upon the ultimate problems of the universe. It is a time for the upward look and trustful silence. Some people are so strong in faith and so sure of God, that they can praise Him in pain, and pass through the valley of the shadow with songs on their lips. But they are rare souls. For most people, it is a time for mute obedience. To fashion a philosophy in such an hour is surely a mistake. If we make it for ourselves, in the time of our *own* tragedy, it will border on despair; if we make it for others, in the hour of *their* grief, it is likely that we shall treat their sorrow too light.

The puerile explanations which amiable people sometimes offer of the dark mysteries in a neighbor's life are shallow indeed. I once heard a benign Christian tell a mother bereaved of her only son that probably God had taken her son away in order to make her more patient. Both the mother and I thought that it was a pitiful attempt at an explanation. The cure seemed so dreadfully out of proportion to the disease. Those who set out "to justify the ways of God to men" need a greater equipment of heart and mind than finds expression here. Better, a thousand times, to hold one's peace than press a motive on God which we would condemn in a man. Someday we expect to pass into His more immediate presence. Can we not willingly accept the mystery of suffering in the meanwhile? Enough light beats upon this dark path for us to pick our way. For the rest, would it not be filial and faithful to wait until we get home, when He will tell us Himself?

I remember that when I was a small boy it was arranged one year that I should go on a two week holiday with my school chums and that no grown-up people should come with us. To our youthful minds, the arrangement seemed ideal. On the night before the holiday began, I counted up my pocket-money and came to the conclusion that it was not enough! So I went to my father about it. He heard my reasonings with a quizzical smile and murmured something about my ignorance of the value of money, but I left quite cheerfully with an understanding in *my* mind that a postal-order would reach me during the second week. And in three days I was ready for the postal-order, so I sent off a post-card to accelerate it. I do not now remember what I put on the card, but I know the *kind* of card it was: "Dear Dad, S.O.S., L.S.D., R.S.V.P."

But this was the queer thing: no answer came. The first week ended and still no answer. The second began and slipped away, and still no answer. My chums noticed my preoccupation and began to explain the absence of the postal-order in their own way. One said, "He has forgotten you're here." I knew that was a lie: I knew my Dad. Another said, "He is too busy to bother with a boy like you." I knew that that was a lie also. A third one said, "What do you think yourself?" I did not know what to think. It was all a mystery to me. "I'll wait until I get home," I said, "and he'll tell me himself."

And when I got home it was all said in two or three sentences. Though I could still feel the sting of it, the look in his eyes was enough. I saw how much he loved me and what it had cost him to discipline his boy, and I have known the value of money ever since.

A Ray of Light Upon a Dark Path

That experience of boyhood has been a parable to me. There are certain dark problems in my family life which I have never been able fully to understand. I had a little sister once; my only sister; the youngest in a family of boys; an angel-child who lived nine years—nine years mostly of pain. Fourteen times in seven years she went to the surgeon's knife until she had no form nor comeliness, and her face was more marred than any man's. At the last, she had to be hidden away. Five gaping wounds yawned in her head alone, and only the strong-nerved could dare to look on what was left of that dear disfigured face.

And some looked and said, "There is no God." And others, well-intentioned but hopelessly incompetent, offered the most shallow explanations. But I was dumb as a boy, and I am dumb as a man. Some light shines upon these dark problems, but no *complete* solution is at hand. I give to enquirers the answer which I gave to my school-chums years ago. "I'll wait until I get home and He'll tell me Himself."

> Someday the silver cord will break,
> And I no more as now shall sing;
> But oh, the joy when I shall wake
> Within the palace of the King!
> And I shall see Him face to face...

And He will tell me Himself! In heaven! In the presence of those who came out of great tribulation! In sight and sound of the army of the redeemed! He will tell me Himself. And I shall be *satisfied* when I awake in heaven. Satisfied.

Meanwhile, we are grateful for every ray of light on this dark path. It is not wholly dark. We see that, in some mysterious way, joy and pain intertwine. They are not really disparate; they belong together. It is a false antithesis which sets them one against the other. They often greet us on the path of life hand in hand. In joy were we conceived, but only by pain and labor were we brought forth. That God-like thing called mother-love was woven in woe.

We see, moreover, how rich a service the sufferers render to our poor tormented race. *Sympathy is a shallow stream in the souls of those who have not suffered.* There is something unheeding and harsh in a man who has known nothing of pain. And sympathy is far too precious in this needy world to begrudge the price at which it must be purchased. When Richard Baxter lost his wife, he declared, in his paroxysm of grief, "I will not be judged by any that never felt the like." It was only another way of saying that he could not be comforted except by those who had. Suffering, in a disciple, can often be wrested to service. It is Christlike work to soothe and sympathize, and only those who have drunk the cup of sorrow are fully equipped to do it.

Furthermore, as we come to understand the family life in which God has placed us on this planet and glimpse the purpose which His loving heart is working out, we come to understand also why we are exposed to grief and pain. Some of it is begotten by ignorance, and some by folly. Omnipotence could have avoided it all, but only at the price of invading our personality and making us marionettes. Can anyone, not utterly engulfed in sorrow, regret that God did not take that path; that His love would not compromise with sin; that He insisted that we bear the penalties of family life as we had enjoyed its privileges; that nothing would thwart Him in His purpose of keeping us in those conditions by which we might attain to the stature of men? Fellowship with God is the fine fruit of this discipline.

> Nearness, likeness to our Lord,
> Our exceeding great reward.

Is it worth it? Aye! Though seven deaths lay between.

Suffering Helps Others

Moreover, to some who suffer physical pain and bear the brunt of dread disease, this further joy is often given. Their suffering helps forward medical research. It may seem a very slight help, simply another one of a thousand "negative instances" but, however slight, if this were true, it would be vicarious. I believe that the mysterious malady which laid hold of my little sister has been better understood by reason of her seven years of pain. An eminent surgeon once said so. Perhaps others have suffered less because she suffered more. Sweet thought! It will add to the joys of heaven for her as she stands before the throne of God, with all those who came out of great tribulation and serve Him day and night in His temple.

Nor must it be forgotten, by any who would have light on suffering, that its power to curse or bless depends upon the reaction of the sufferer. Observant men in all ages have noticed that the same trouble in two lives has produced precisely opposite results. One is strangely sweetened, refined, enriched. Another is embittered, jaundiced, and made sour. The same distress! One suffered it willingly, dared to believe that God could wrest even from this ugly intruder something worth the price pain paid, sobbed it out on the Savior's breast, but went on in brave faith. The other spoke bitter words, accused God, and took up arms against heaven. Even if the truth of their opposed philosophies could be left aside as both, at present, unproven, one thing at least is proven beyond a shadow of honest doubt. The first live a happier, fuller, and much more useful life, and they are, moreover, much more pleasant to live *with*. Even if the reverent reasoning of the problem did not lead us to a willing acceptance of such woe as are, at present, inevitable; utility, other people's happiness, and our own peace of mind, ought to do so.

I well remember a member of my congregation coming to my door one day in deep distress. Her daughter had recently been admitted as a patient to the eye hospital and had gone in with every hope of recovery. But the disease proved more deadly than anyone guessed, and, on the day when my visitor stumbled over my step, the blow had fallen. The doctors foresaw that she would be blind in three weeks or a month and suggested that it would be best, if the mother broke the news to her girl. She, poor soul, had come to pass the terrible task on to me. I went with lagging footsteps to the hospital, and I can see the little private ward now as I saw it then. The single bed, the locker, the polished floor, the drawn blind, and the patient turning her fast dimming eyes towards me. I talked of trivialities for some minutes, scheming for an opening, and half afraid that she would hear my thumping heart. Then she guessed! Perhaps I paused too long, or she divined it by some vibrant note in my voice, for suddenly she burst out with a half-suppressed sob, "Oh! I believe that God is going to take my sight away."

It was a hideous moment and an ugly phrase. My divided heart in that minute was half in prayer to God and half in talk with her. I remembered a story I had heard of a missionary in India and what he said when he lost his little girl and I said: "Jessie, I wouldn't let Him;" and when she begged me to explain, I falteringly asked if she thought (not at once, but in three weeks or a month!) she could pray a prayer like this: "Father, if for any reason known to Thee, I must lose my sight, I will not let it be taken from me. I will give it to Thee."

And in three weeks or a month, she prayed that prayer. It was not easy. Does any half-wit think it was? One day she clutched at my hand and declared that she simply could not live in this world without a bit of light, but she offered the prayer as the last glimpse of day vanished forever. Peace came with the prayer. She carries the cross willingly, not grudgingly, or of necessity, but with a cheerful courage. She is sweet to live with, and God uses her for the comfort and help of others.

The task of the minister is not easy. Every week brings its batch of difficult duties, and there are times when the spirit rebels. A succession of sad stories, and constant contact with sudden tragedy and writhing pain, drains one of nervous energy and drives one to perplexed prayer. Sometimes the prayers become complaints. We tell Jesus irreverently, and petulantly, that we cannot go to poor tormented people who are submerged in repeated sorrows, and talk about a God of Love. And always, in such an hour, when the spirit is overwhelmed and the ministry insupportable, Jesus comes and shows us His wounds.

> The dear tokens of His passion
> Still His dazzling body bears.

Poor dumb mouths! If those wounds could only speak . . . ! Yet, in their silence, they are mighty and draw the soul out through the eyes in hot, adoring love.

> With what rapture,
> *With what rapture*
> Gaze we on those glorious scars.

It is enough. He is able!—able to succor the sufferers, for He has suffered Himself; able to sustain His ministers and make them into living flame; able to support the wavering faith of those who are tormented with doubt through all the long night in which the mystery hangs, until, at last, He brings all His faithful into God's holy presence, and, in the light and joy of heaven, the Father will tell us Himself.

TEXTUAL INDEX

The reading of these sermons will enrich your life, and enhance your skills as an interpreter, teacher, and communicator of God's truth.

CLASSIC SERMONS ON THE ATTRIBUTES OF GOD

Powerful sermons by highly acclaimed pulpit masters lay a solid foundation for growing in the knowledge of God. Rediscover the profound truths revealed in His attributes, such as His: terribleness and gentleness, mercy, knowability, sovereignty, jealousy, omnipresence, immutability, comfort, greatness, omniscience, and love.

You will be inspired and challenged by these great sermons from such famous preachers as: J. D. Jones, George H. Morrison, Dwight L Moody, Henry Ward Beecher, Arthur J. Gossip, John H. Jowett, J. Stewart Holden, Joseph Parker, Frederick W. Robertson, Charles H. Spurgeon, and John Wesley.

CLASSIC SERMONS ON FAITH AND DOUBT

Twelve pulpit giants give you inspiration and devotional challenge for your faith in this book of sermons. These messages to stimulate your faith are from the pulpit ministry of John H. Jowett, D. Martyn Lloyd-Jones, Martin Luther, G. Campbell Morgan, John Wesley and others. Preachers and lay persons alike will be encouraged and find great blessing in these forceful messages.

CLASSIC SERMONS ON PRAYER

Pulpit giants Dwight L Moody, G. Campbell Morgan, Charles H. Spurgeon, Rueben A. Torrey, Alexander Whyte, and others, present the need, the how-to, and the results of a life that is permeated with prayer. These classic sermons on prayer will energize your prayer life, show you how to expect great things from God, and help you experience the strengthening power of God in your everyday life.

CLASSIC SERMONS ON THE PRODIGAL SON

These sermons by highly acclaimed pulpit masters offer unique insights into perhaps the most famous of Christ's parables. Famous pulpiteers such as J. Wilbur Chapman, D. Martyn Lloyd-Jones, Alexander Maclaren, D. L. Moody, George H. Morrison, Charles H. Spurgeon, Joseph Parker, Frederick W. Robertson, and Alexander Whyte offer masterful interpretations and life-changing applications of this marvelous portion of Scripture.

These sermons will provide new understanding of the relationships between the son, father and the other son. Readers will be especially comforted with the wonderful truth of the Father's love as it is skillfully applied to the issues of life in these classic sermons.

CLASSIC SERMONS ON WORSHIP

Rediscover the beauty of worship! In this day of renewed appreciation for biblical worship, believers need to hear the resounding voices of some of God's greatest Bible communicators from the past. This exciting collection of *Classic Sermons* will help Christians understand what the Bible says about worship, and will motivate us to apply these vital truths to our lives and churches.

TREASURY OF THE WORLD'S GREATEST SERMONS

123 sermons by many of the world's most notable preachers of ancient and modern days, compiled by Warren W. Wiersbe.

A Sermon Library in One Volume!

Great pulpit princes and their sermon masterpieces are organized and presented here, together with dates and indexes of authors, sermon topics and Bible texts. They illustrate variety of gifts and diversity of methods, together with national and ecclesiastical peculiarities.

This list of great preachers includes theologians such as John Calvin and Jonathan Edwards; evangelists such as Christmas Evans; and pulpiteers such as Charles H. Spurgeon, G. Campbell Morgan, and Alexander Maclaren.

Progress is shown in the art of preaching. Although all have literary and rhetorical excellence, each sermon contains a distinct message helpful in solving present-day problems in Christian living. Each one is representative of the preaching that characterized the age to which it belongs.

"Every minister should be a reader," writes Warren W. Wiersbe. Himself an ardent reader of sermons and biographies, he recommends that every minister read the giants—the great writers and preachers of all centuries—both what they have written and their biographies.

For variety and solid content, *The Treasury of the World's Great Sermons* is a superior collection.

Available from your local Christian bookstore, or

KREGEL *Publications*

P.O. Box 2607, Grand Rapids, MI 49501